Exploring Our Lutheran Liturgy

Dennis R. Fakes

CSS Publishing Company, Inc.
Lima, Ohio

Library Of Congress Cataloging-in-Publication Data

Fakes, Dennis R., 1948-
   Exploring our Lutheran liturgy / Dennis R. Fakes.
      p.   cm.
   Includes bibliographical references.
   ISBN 1-55673-596-0
   1. Lutheran Church—Liturgy. I. Title.
BX8067.A1F35   1994
264'.041—dc20   93-42323
                                               CIP

ISBN 1-55673-596-0   PRINTED IN U.S.A.

Dedicated to
Hilda
who daily teaches me the meaning of Grace

Table Of Contents

Preface

I have always been troubled by formal worship. Something deep within me says, "This is important" and yet so often I find myself merely mouthing words of worship devoid of meaning. I feel guilty and hypocritical and yet the informal services I have attended, usually in other denominations, leave me cold. I like the Lutheran liturgy.

Many people who worship at Lutheran churches have no idea what they are doing. They don't know the meaning of the words, the significance of the actions, or the value of the music as these things work together with architecture, art, vestments, and the building itself to draw human beings closer to God. I suspect this is why a survey of Lutherans revealed that 50 percent think of Sunday worship as boring. Many young people, never having studied Lutheran worship, will find no comparison between the Lutheran liturgies and MTV. Worship is boring, unless we understand with our hearts and our minds the drama and richness of Lutheran worship.

At the request of the worship and music committee of my church and in response to my own felt need for greater understanding and knowledge, and to do what I could to make worship more meaningful, I wrote a series of sermons at Messiah Lutheran Church, Lindsborg, Kansas, based on liturgy. The response was quite favorable. My worship depth increased and the members of the congregation told me week after week how much they picked up and appreciated learning about what they had been doing, in some cases, for decades.

I treated the various sections of the liturgy devotionally — as if they were sermon texts. I wanted to relate the action of the liturgy with the daily lives of the people. My weekly intention was to communicate the gospel through the liturgy. That is my purpose in this book as well. What does the good news of Jesus Christ have to say to us as we worship? It is our Triune

God who initiates worship by moving us to faith. God is the chief liturgist. Our Creator God brings us to life; our Redeemer God brings us to eternal life; our Sanctifier God brings us to renewal of life.

My sincere hope is that this book enriches Lutheran worship. I love this church and its liturgy and know that something valuable is weekly unappreciated by millions of us. This book can be used as a guide by a pastor, wishing to do what I did in acquainting (or perhaps re-acquainting) the congregation to Lutheran worship. It may also be used devotionally by clergy and laity alike in personal or family devotions. It can also be used in classes on worship and the liturgy. And, of course, it can be read as one might read any book. Whatever way it may be used, my prayer is that the gospel grow in each heart, mind and soul and that the community of God's people, the church, grow in holy love for God and each other.

Since there are so many similar elements in the two prominent Lutheran worship books today, *Lutheran Worship* and the *Lutheran Book Of Worship*, I have included both in this study. I follow the *Lutheran Book Of Worship* format when there is a difference in order between the books.

Introduction

A retired pastor friend told me about his first church in Colorado. "I had a large, very active family in the church. They were all active, that is, except the husband and father. So I went to see him one day. 'Pastor,' he said to me, 'I don't come to church because of some of the things that happen in the Lutheran Church. If you'll just sit on that barrel there, I'll tell you all about the things I don't like." I said to him, "Why don't you come to my new member class I'm starting this week and learn about why we do things the way we do, and then I'll sit on that barrel and hear what you don't like. Perhaps if you understand why we do the things we do, they wouldn't be so objectionable to you."

The man took up the pastor's offer and went to the new member class. Now he understood that when the minister turned his back to him in worship, it was not because of rudeness and insensitivity — there was a reason for it. Having the people rise for the reading of the Gospel was not arbitrary crowd control. The apparent rigidity of the service had reasons. The various other formalities of the worship service now made sense. The result was that this man received instruction, was baptized, and became a very active member of the congregation. Some years later the pastor overheard this man telling some of the long-time Lutherans about the worship service, "I didn't know that's why we did that," some of them said at various times as this relative newcomer explained the Lutheran liturgy to them.

The Lutheran Church is a liturgical church. "Liturgical" means formal worship — following a prescribed order. The literal meaning of "liturgical" is "people work" — the work of the people in worshiping God. Paul H. D. Lang described liturgy as "the church's worship as distinguished from private, personal, and group devotions."[1]

9

Why have a liturgal service? Why not "just let the Spirit move" the people in worship as many critics of the Lutheran liturgy suggest? "Wouldn't it be more meaningful if the words came from the heart rather than from a worship book?" Apparently the Corinthian Christians thought the same — and it tore the church apart! Paul advised, "all things should be done decently and in order." (1 Corinthians 14:40)[2] A formal liturgy developed very early in the life of the church for those coming together to worship the living God.

There certainly is meaning in individual worship and prayer and this has always been encouraged in the Lutheran Church. But for public worship, the individual becomes part of a larger group — the universal, "catholic" church of all time, space, ethnic background, language, tradition, and so forth. In formal, public worship, the individual is absorbed into something far larger than his or her singular boundaries. Here the individual becomes part of the mystical body of Christ. Here the past traditions (and usually words and even music) are preserved as a symbol of the larger church beyond the individual, congregation, district, synod, denominational body, or nationality.

The liturgy reminds us that we are connected not only to those who worshiped in the many generations before us, but it also connects us to heaven itself and the church triumphant. As the preface before Holy Communion says, "And so, with the Church on earth and the hosts of heaven, we praise your name and join their unending hymn: Holy, holy, holy Lord, God of pow'r and might: Heaven and earth are full of your glory. Hosanna, Hosanna, Hosanna in the highest. Blessed is he who comes in the name of the Lord. Hosanna in the highest."

The liturgy is the gift of the Holy Spirit and not formulated by some committee. Neither is it the offspring of some creative and gifted writer. In a real sense the liturgy is the response of people moved by the Spirit as revealed and tested through time, tradition, and faith. There is great comfort knowing that the Lutheran liturgy springs from all that is good of the past.

And yet the language is ours — unique for our time and subject to the changing needs of future generations. As Paul Zeller Strodach has written, the liturgy "has grown with the centuries. The piety of all wise and pious. It has grown with the centuries. The piety of all times has tested it, added what was worthy, cleansed it from what was unworthy. The fragrant incense of a ceaseless devotion of multitudes to the Saviour comes to us with the Liturgy."[3]

Furthermore, our outward ceremonies testify and reflect our inner beliefs. If I love my family, I will likely participate in certain family rituals that convey my individual love. I will be present as the family gathers for Thanksgiving turkey, Christmas turkey and Easter ham. The rituals of my daily existence will tell of my inner love. I may nightly tuck my children to bed and kiss my spouse before going to sleep. Mere ritual — sometimes and yet never "mere." Always my ritual is important because it reveals my inner beliefs and values. An ancient Latin formula puts it this way: *Lex orandi lex credendi.* "As we worship so we believe" or "as we believe so we worship."

Chapter One

Lutheran Worship

Authentic worship has the effect of a love affair between the worshiper and God. Too often, however, it looks more like the marriage proposal made by a very respectable New Englander in Amherst, Massachusetts, recorded more than 160 years ago. He told the young lady that he had been measuring her in his mind and that, with some minor changes, she might fill the place as his wife. He wrote:

> *I hope I have no foolishness called romance. I am much too well balanced for that sort of nonsense, but we might look forward to leading a respectable and useful life and enjoy the esteem of our neighbors.*

Wouldn't a proposal like that sweep you off your feet? Yet that proposal is a fair picture of what many of us Lutherans pass off as our worship of Jesus Christ. There's no passion involved. It's strictly head-stuff.

We worship because the human soul seems to need the presence of God. We worship with the greater communion of saints because they remind each of us of a larger reality. Coming together in a place of worship lifts us from the normal. Participating in ancient ritual and contemporary prayer; looking to the parousia — the end of all things — gives us an optimal picture of reality that includes time and space as well as eternity. God is present in worship. Most people sense that. People often say so. People often say they feel nearest to God on Sunday mornings and in a church building.

The Lutheran faith is based on "justification by grace through faith." Worship must convey Christ — the good news. If worship does not give us the very freedom of the gospel, then it is not authentic worship. Too many experiences called "worship" are little more than guilt trips and manipulation. The guilt can work two ways: one feels guilty for not going to worship (even though worship is not liberating), or one feels guilty as a result of worship and the manipulation of a worship leader to do, think or be something other than what one is now doing, thinking or being. One can emerge from worship feeling shame, worthlessness, and filthy rather than free, worthy, and whole. Authentic Lutheran worship is centered around the glorious good news of Jesus Christ. Nothing less, nothing more.

We worship in awe and reverence before the almighty God. As Moses removed his sandals because of the holy ground, so we put forth our best. As the writer to the Hebrews says, "We offer God an acceptable worship with reverence and awe; for indeed our God is a consuming fire." (Hebrews 12:28b-29) This sense of holiness — otherness — leads us to bow before the Lord our God in appropriate worship. We stand for the reading of the gospel and at various other parts of the liturgy where we wish to show our respect for the living Lord (usually during the parts associated with prayer and praise). The congregation sits for instruction.

Our love of God leads to our worship. We love God first and then our neighbors as ourselves. Therefore we do nothing to offend our neighbor in our worship. As Paul writes, "Let all things be done for building up" (1 Corinthians 14:26b), especially our worship. It is in this context of love that Paul challenges the church to let all things be done "decently and in order." (1 Corinthians 14:39b) For many making the sign of the cross is a reminder of God's love received and given in return. Our love prompts us in our giving to share as we have received.

Humility is certainly appropriate in our worship. There is no room for vaulting the self and lessening others. Certainly worship is in God's house and this is the time to lay aside our individuality and come together as the people of God to worship the God of all. We humbly acknowledge our Creator by standing at various parts of the liturgy to give God honor and especially by kneeling to show our respect and acknowledgment of our status under God.

The minister faces the altar when addressing God and the congregation when approaching the people. With free-standing altars it is often possible to face both altar and people. A general rule is that when the minister stands before the altar, it is for all *sacrificial* acts and the congregation for all *sacramental* acts. Here "sacrificial" means those parts directed at God; "sacramental" means those which are directed to the congregation. Between parts the minister, helpers, and choir face either sides of the church building (but not the congregation).

The various actions combine with the words to draw us closer to our God. In the Lutheran service people sometimes joke that all the standing, sitting, standing, sitting, kneeling is better than an aerobic workout tape. Such postures are deliberate — although not ancient. Standing was the normal position for worship in the church for 1,000 years. (So be thankful that you do get to sit from time to time and that the church has adapted to modern needs.) The early Christians stood to symbolize that they had risen with Christ. Standing also symbolized the joy Christians felt. St. Irenaeus (A.D. 180) mentions the custom of standing for worship and says it derives from apostolic authority. Even today standing should be the most usual posture of worship (even though few Lutherans see it that way). There is a constant temptation to want to be entertained and to take a passive position toward worship and "peoples' work" (liturgy). Such is not the case in Lutheran worship.

Sitting in worship was not allowed until St. Augustine in the fourth century. Then it was only for the sermon. There were no seats available for the people anyway. So if they chose not to stand, the had only the floor to recline upon. Many ancient churches such as the Church of the Nativity in Bethlehem or the Church of the Holy Sepulchre in Jerusalem still have no pews.

The Building

The place where most of us worship is in a church building. Here architecture and art combine to point the believer God-ward. Sometimes this is done quite well; other times — not.

In the early days of the church, the believers met in the synagogue or in homes. Later, as the church gained acceptance, pagan temples were used for church buildings. Over time, architectural styles developed that served to point the human soul toward its encounter with the divine.

The church building has three main parts: the *narthex* or vestibule, the *nave* or central part or main body — where the people sit, and the *chancel* — where the altar is located.

Many of our Lutheran churches are in congruence with the effort to orient the church so that the members of the congregation face east to worship. From the east the "Day-spring from on high" arose. The rising sun reminds the worshiper of The True Light of the world. Even if the building is not literally facing east, the direction of worship is still called east.

After entering through the *Narthex*, people sit in the *Nave*. The church is often compared to a ship sailing over the sea of time. If *Nave* looks and sounds a lot like *Navy*, that is the reason. Using one's imagination, if you turn a church's *Nave* upside down, it resembles the bow of a boat. The most important item in the *Nave* would appear to be the pews or chairs where the congregation sits. That is not the case, however. The most important piece of furniture is the *baptismal font*. It ranks in importance with the altar and the pulpit in the chancel. The *baptismal font* gets its importance from the sacrament. Holy baptism is the means by which one enters the congregation and family of God. The vessel of baptism, the font, is therefore placed in a prominent position. In many congregations it is positioned near the door (to remind each person entering the building of his or her baptism). Usually it is placed near the chancel (for convenience, especially during a baptism).

The worshiping community faces the chancel (the word comes from *cancelli,* which means screens). One can best understand the name by visiting an Eastern Orthodox church. There the screens remain. There is an actual, physical dividing line between the things of God and the people of God. Today there are Lutheran churches that have a rail dividing the spaces. Such a dividing line, separating officiating clergy from worshipers, is not evangelical. It is used primarily for receiving the sacrament of the Altar. Kneeling to receive the sacrament became common during the Middle Ages. Prior to that communicants received the Sacrament standing up.

Incidentally, the place where the altar is located is called the *Sanctuary*. Many times people use the term "sanctuary" to describe the interior of the church building. While the word has a technical meaning for those of us in the church, most people use "sanctuary" to describe a holy place such as a church, chapel, or place where one can retreat to be near God. Many use "sanctuary" as a place of refuge or protection. In Old Testament days a refugee from people seeking revenge would find protection in God's house.

The room adjoining the chancel is called the *Sacristy*. This is the room of preparation. The vestments and altar hangings are stored here as well as other items such as candles, linens, crucifix, and so forth. The minister uses the sacristy for prayer prior to worship.

When I was a boy, our family had a gathering in the basement of the local Methodist church. We had a meal and then everyone sat around and visited. But I got bored and snuck upstairs to the nave. My eyes were filled with wonder at the large stained glass windows — one of Jesus standing outside a door with hand raised in a knocking gesture; the second window portraying Jesus with a lamb in his arms and other sheep peaceably looking up to the Great Shepherd of the sheep. But what really caught my eye was the chancel area — the forbidden zone. I had never been in the chancel of a church. Mystery and holiness filled the place. I slowly walked to the front, took a deep breath, and stepped up that first step. So far, so good. Lightning hadn't struck and there was no perceptible trembling of the earth — yet! And then I moved to the pulpit and actually stepped behind it for the first time in my life.

I felt guilty, but also felt a profound sense of awe and mystery. This was a holy place. I sensed it deep within my spirit.

The church building IS a holy place! It was set aside for a unique purpose: the worship of God. In an effort to make churches more economical, the space is often used for concerts and meetings. Children think nothing of playing in the chancel area. I sense that the building has lost something of its set-apartness, its uniqueness.

The building is, to some extent, modeled after the temple in Jerusalem. The nave is for the common worshiper. The chancel is for the clergy as the inner sanctuary of the temple was reserved only for the priestly tribe. The chancel containing the holy altar, is God's just as in the temple — although now it is open. (Remember the curtain in the temple was torn when Jesus died. This torn curtain symbolized the direct access we have to God.) Even ordained clergy must enter the chancel with reverence, awe, respect. This place is uniquely God's space.

The best and finest the congregation can afford is used in God's house: gold, brass, silk, solid wood, real flowers, beeswax candles. And, while the practice seems to be changing in the Lutheran Church, we wear only our best on Sundays as well. God gets the best of us!

The altar in the chancel is the center of attention in most Lutheran churches. Long before there were churches or even the temple in Jerusalem, God's people worshiped around an altar. Harkening back to the early chapter of Genesis, "Cain brought to the LORD an offering of the fruit of the ground, and Abel for his part brought of the firstlings of his flock ..." (Genesis 4:3-4) These sacrifices surely involved an altar.

The altar serves several purposes. It is the Lord's table and from it the elements of the sacrament are distributed. In 1 Corinthians (10:21) the "table of the Lord" is where believers gather around to share the Lord's supper. In this way the Christian "table of the Lord" is unlike the pagan altar where only sacrifices are offered.

It is also an emblem of sacrifice as were the very first altars. The very word altar comes from the Latin *altare ara,* which means an elevated place for sacrifice. Here believers lift up their hearts to the supreme sacrifice — the very Son of God. Believers lift up their sacrifice of prayer, praise, thanksgiving, and symbols of themselves — usually money, bread and wine.

Finally, the altar is the emblem of God's presence. Here is where God and God's people meet. As the flag is the symbol of our country, so the altar is the sign of our faith. This is why the altar is the center of attention in the church building. We allow nothing to detract from it.

A crucifix is the most prominent object above or on the altar. It represents the sacrificial element that the altar conveys. Our Lord died and the visual token of his body on the cross reminds the congregation of the tremendous cost of grace. An empty cross represents the resurrected Christ. Either a crucifix or an empty cross is appropriate.

Candles must be real. Candles on or behind the altar represent God as the light and help convey the presence of God in the assembly of the believers. Candles especially represent Christ as the light of the world. The burning candles embody sacrifice as they burn themselves in order to shed light. The number of candles used may vary with the church year: the simple services using the fewer candles while the more festive services having more. Candles on the epistle side of the altar are lit first (on the right as you face the altar). The one closest to the cross is lit first and extinguished last.

Other candles are often used in our churches. A *sanctuary lamp* is placed in the sanctuary, near the altar, and kept burning seven days a week, 24 hours a day. The candle is usually replaced weekly. Often the sanctuary lamp is suspended from the ceiling. The glass may be clear, white or colored. There is no liturgical significance to the glass.

A *Paschal candle* is a large white candle on a floor candlestick which is lighted on Easter Eve and lit for each service until the ascension service. At the ascension it is extinguished and removed after the words of the gospel have been read: "He was taken up into heaven." This candle is symbolic of Christ's rising from the dead and his ministry on earth from the resurrection until his ascension. Five grains of incense are inserted as marks of the five wounds of our Lord. The current year of our Lord is usually engraved on the candle. It is placed on the gospel side of the altar, except when at baptisms and funerals (the other two occasions when this candle is used).

Baptism candles are given to those baptized as a symbol of the light of faith received in the sacrament of Holy Baptism. The candle burns and is consumed as the baptized person's life is consumed in Christian service. The minister says, "Let your light so shine before others that they may see your good works and glorify your Father in heaven" when this candle is given to the baptized (usually through a sponsor in the case of infant baptism).

The *altar linens* point to the burial (again the sacrifice) of Christ. Their presence on the altar suggest the burial cloths left in the empty tomb. When the altar is stripped on Maundy Thursday, the bare altar reminds us of Christ's humiliation and of the slab upon which his body was laid in the tomb. The various linens used for baptism and holy communion also have great symbolic value. The *Corporal* for example is a square of very fine linen upon which the sacramental vessels are placed. The name says a great deal, as does the *Pall* which is used to cover the chalice.

Altar hangings change with the church year. White is the color of the high festivals and their seasons. Red is used for Pentecost and minor festivals, violet for the penitential season of Lent and blue for the Advent preparation season. Green suggests growth and is used on the ordinary days following Epiphany and Pentecost. Black may be used on Good Friday.

When most people think of church buildings, they automatically think of steeples, stained glass windows, and bells. Anthropologists have noted that often we human beings place our most prominent institutions in the most conspicuous of places, usually giving the buildings representing these institutions the highest stature. In ancient Egypt, the pyramids represented the power of the pharaohs, for example. During the rule of the Romans, the Coliseum and the Forum were quite conspicuous. Likewise, during the middle ages, when the church held the power, its buildings were ornate, large, and tall. The steeple stood out as the tallest structure in the community. It pointed heaven-ward and reminded everyone in symbolic ways that God's church represented that higher place and power.

If *steeples* are the visual symbol of a greater reality, bells are the auditory. They give clear summons to worship and prayer. *Bells* are powerful reminders of God's presence. They call the people to repentance, worship, praying the Lord's Prayer, rejoicing at marriages, and mourning at funerals. The voices of bells were so strong in medieval times that they were often considered living creatures. They were baptized and even given names.

In modern urban society, church bells have been relegated to one of many sounds heard in our noisy streets, if heard at all. Most Lutheran churches being built today do not have real bells. If anything, they use an electronic clarion system. There are some congregations in rural communities where bells remain as important aids to worship.

Stained-glass windows began in the 11th century and beautifully illustrated the stories of the Bible that were not available to lay people who could neither read nor gain access to the few books available. In brilliant colors the windows proclaimed God's glory and power. The windows reached out and grabbed the viewer's attention. Even today, some churches have powerful windows that effectively teach the old story. Who has not, as a child, stood before a brilliant stained-glass window and marveled at the colors?

Today most people can read. The Bible stories are repeated again and again. People know them and no longer need to learn visually with stained glass as teachers. The print media teaches more effectively than lead and glass. But the lure of stained-glass beauty remains an important part of many churches — Protestant and Roman Catholic.

Vestments

Vestments are the unique articles of clothing ministers wear for worship. The wearing of vestments is an ancient practice reaching back into the Old Testament (cf. Exodus 28 where the priests' ceremonial vestments were divinely appointed).

I have seen some movement in my lifetime in this area. Growing up I remember the minister always wearing a long, black robe and sometimes wearing a *stole* (the colored band of cloth worn around the neck and down the front). When I entered seminary, I also purchased a long, black robe, called in this case, a *cassock*. Over the cassock I wore a *surplice,* a loose-fitting white garment that did not quite cover the cassock. Being a seminarian, I was not eligible for wearing the stole because it represents ordination. At ordination I received a red stole as a symbol of the yoke of Christ I assumed as an ordained minister of the church. The minister usually wears the stole hanging straight from the shoulders although it can be worn crossed over the breast. A deacon may wear a single stole over the left shoulder. The stole is always the color of the day: Green, for example, on the Sundays of Epiphany or the Sundays after Pentecost.

In my second church I purchased an *alb* and have worn an alb ever since. The alb (from the Latin *Alba* meaning white) is a long robe that is white (or off-white) — never colored. A cassock is not worn under it. The alb resembles the surplice except that it is longer and more complete. It may be worn by all the ministers of the service, whether ordained or not, including minister, assisting ministers, choir members, and so forth. It suggests the baptismal gown worn as a symbol of our being clothed in the righteousness of Christ. The alb is bound around the middle by a rope or cloth called a cincture.

The final vestment is the *chasuble* — a poncho-like robe worn for the celebration of holy communion. It is the most distinctive ancient Eucharistic vestment of the church.

This evolution in official clergy wear for divine worship has happened over the last few decades in the Lutheran Church in the United States. This is truly a new and positive development in our church. From the Reformation until the middle of this century, most Lutherans did what they could to distance themselves from things Roman Catholic. Lutheran ministers, after all, are not priests and therefore should not look like priests. Throughout much of our history the black gown seemed to be the vestment most universally worn by Lutheran ministers. Its roots, like the roots of the Reformation itself, is in academia. The gown was modeled after academic dress, specifically the doctor's gown. The cassock derived from the medieval black robe, which in its earliest origins was an undergarment and not a liturgical vestment at all.

When a bit of doctrine or practice is not essential to salvation, we use the word "adiaphora." Vestments have been considered "adiaphora" for some time and, unfortunately, when something is adiaphora, it is often under-emphasized. Finally, now in this later 20th century, the Reformation has come full circle with vestments.

The true church vestments derive their origins from the Bible itself. They were the everyday garb of the earliest celebrants of the divine liturgy. Several times the New Testament mentinons a *tunic* (Matthew 5:40; 10:9f; John 19:23; Revelation 1:13) It was a full cut robe which was gathered at the neck and which extended to the ankles. The narrow sleeves reached the wrists. This is the garment we now call the Alb. This makes the alb the oldest and most universally used *vestment.*

To keep warm, the people in biblical times wore an overcoat. (2 Timothy 4:13) This cloak was usually of one piece of material, cut round or elliptical in shape, with a hole in the center for the head. It was made of heavy linen, or cloth. Because it enveloped the entire body it was soon called the *casula,* "little house;" from this we get the word chasuble. Like the tunic (alb), it became a distinctive part of liturgical wear by the fourth century or earlier.

The *chasuble* is the principal vestment for the presiding minister during the celebration of the holy communion. The "little house" symbolizes the all-embracing meal the pastor presides over. All of God's people are invited to this thanksgiving meal.

An early garment in common use was the rather long, oblong napkin, carried over the left shoulder. This garment was first used in the East in worship as it was waved back and forth by servers to drive away insects. Then it was adopted as a distinctive mark of the priest and the deacon. After some centuries it came into the use of the western church as the *stole,* the distinctive mark of ordination.

Music

Anybody can see that music is an important part of the Lutheran liturgy. I once had an organist who was an accountant by profession and an "organist" on the side. He was terrible! His "music" was noise and the church suffered horribly from his refusal to practice and give God his very best. The church in which I was raised was very small and my sister played the organ. She was no organist and made no pretensions to be an organist. It was just that she was the only person who could play any musical instrument out of our group of 20 or so people. She gave it her best, but even she would admit — it wasn't so great.

Music is the great handicap of the Lutheran liturgy for many in similar, limited situations. And, as often happens with handicaps, music is also the great strength of the Lutheran liturgy — especially when done right and in glory to God alone.

The pastor is in charge of the music as well as everything else in the liturgy. The minister may not be a musician (I certainly am not!), but that does not relieve clergy of responsibility for hiring capable people, persuading the church council to pay adequate salaries for church musicians to attract qualified people, and final judgment regarding what music is or is not appropriate. The buck stops here, for the pastor in all matters of worship — including music.

Paul H. D. Lang, in his book *Ceremony And Celebration*, outlines three principles for good church music:

First Principle — Liturgical music must be objective in character. It must be directed to God and not to people. Here art is employed to the glory of God alone. This is not time for the glory of the musician, whether singer, organist, or choir. Concert music is not appropriate precisely because it is usually not directed to the glory of God alone. Likewise sentimental music, which is subjective in character, is not appropriate. The music may be ever so beautiful and meaningful, but if it is not to the glory of God, it has no place in divine worship.

J. S. Bach, one of the greatest of all Lutheran composers, initialed each piece of music he wrote with S. D. G. which meant *soli dei gloria* — to the glory of God alone. This is a most appropriate attitude for every church musician and for each piece of music chosen. This principle also gives us a good reason to have the musicians out of sight.

Second Principle — The music is to be an aid to worshipers in receiving God's grace. Here the mood may be for sorrow or joy, adoration or praise. The music helps draw the worshiper

from the concerns and cares of the world as well as the preoc-
cupation with self to the seat of God's grace and glory. Good
church music is a handmaid and not the object of worship.
It, like John the Baptist, points beyond to the greater Reality.

Third Principle — Worship music must be sacred music
— as distinguished from secular or worldly. I have seen this
principle violated most frequently in weddings. The bride and
groom seem to think the wedding service is their service and
not a service of the church. "Therefore," they conclude, "we
should be able to choose the music we want." And the popular culture has some very secular music it deems as appropriate
when it really is not. As beautiful as it is, Wagner's *Wedding
March* from *Lohengrin* is really not a wedding march, but a
sensuous dance into the bedroom in which the bridegroom
murders a rival and finally abandons his bride! Appropriate
music? Not really. Many contemporary tunes such as *Sunrise,
Sunset* from *Fiddler on the Roof*, and *Wedding Song* by Paul
Stookie are nice songs about weddings and the feelings sur-
rounding this important life event, but usually not appropriate
for worship.

Music is so important to the Lutheran liturgy, that it makes
or breaks the service itself. The church musician and the people responsible for the music have enormous power and responsibility. Their ministry is critical. Music that is inappropriate
or done poorly or for self-glorification, is unsuitable for divine worship. Indifference, ignorance, and popular waves often
carry more weight in our services than they should. Sometimes
musicians feel the pastor has no right to tell them what is right
or not. Sometimes the people in the pew have their own beliefs with little or no consideration for the broader implications for worship.

The Church Year

Many Lutherans are only vaguely aware there is such a thing
as a "church year." It began in the early days of the church.

Then it was a simple pattern consisting of only two elements: Sunday, the day of Resurrection and *Pascha* (Greek for "Passover"), the annual anniversary of Jesus' death and resurrection, which had taken place at the time of the Jewish Passover.

Gradually more elements were added to this basic pattern: in the third century, the annual Pascha had extended into a 50-day period of festal joy called *Pentecost*. Pentecost also is a Jewish celebration: the Feast of Weeks, falling 50 days after Passover. "Pentecost" comes from the Greek, meaning 50th.

Dramatic changes came to the church in the fourth century as Christianity moved from being a sect to a legally recognized faith and eventually the established religion of the Roman empire. Worship went public — often occupying the pagan temples. The ceremonies became more elaborate to match the settings. The paschal season expanded with Lent, Holy Week, and the Ascension. The new festivals of Christmas and Epiphany were added to replace the deeply-rooted pagan celebration of the festival of the Sun, in recognition of the winter solstice. Now they had something to celebrate: the Sun of Righteousness — Jesus Christ. (There is another possible explanation for choosing December 25 as the day of Christ's birth [the actual date is forever lost]: Hippolytus [c. 220 A.D.] had calculated March 25 as the date of crucifixion. The early Christians may have associated Jesus' conception with the date of his death. Thus December 25 is exactly nine months after his death on March 25).

Through the centuries various Saint's days and festivals were added. Luther asserted that the liturgical cycle of feasts and fasts were neither necessary for salvation nor an obstacle to it. He did, however, regard the church year as a useful vehicle for God's word. That is why the Lutheran churches retained the church year.

The smallest unit in the church year is the day. With each day, the less liturgical services of *Morning Prayer, Evening Prayer, Responsive Prayer, the Litany*, and *Propers for Daily Prayer* are all available for our use. The Reformation originally intended that Christians would worship daily. This practice, however, fell into disfavor during the 18th and 19th centuries.

There are four levels of days on the church year calendar. The *Principal Festivals* always take precedence over any other day or observance. The principal festivals are Christmas Day, Epiphany, Easter Day, Ascension, Pentecost, and Trinity Sunday. Then there are *Sundays and Days of Special Devotion* such as Ash Wednesday and the days of Holy Week. The third level consists of the days of the Apostles, Evangelists, and certain other New Testament people and events. These are the *Lesser Festivals*. Finally the least festive unit consists of the *Commemorations* celebrating diverse biblical people and significant personalities from other times.

The second unit of the church year is the week. Each week begins with the Lord's Day, *Sunday*. Sunday is not the Sabbath, as many people believe. The Sabbath is literally the seventh day — Saturday. The Lord's day is the day set aside to commemorate what happened on that day many years ago. It was on that day, the eighth-day of creation that Christ rose from the dead. This is why Sundays are not counted as part of the 40 days of Lent.

The month is not part of the church year. The next largest section is the *season* of the church year. The various seasons are most commonly recognized by the changing colors (just as the natural seasons of the year are marked by the colors of nature). The church year is a cycle or circle that re-enacts the life of our Lord and the life of God's people and tells the story again and again.

The rhythm of the natural year is included in the church year. Advent, for example, is during the time of the year when the days grow their shortest and, for those in the northern hemisphere, when the weather is usually chilly to cold. This season of repentance reminds the worshiper of the coldness of death and the shortness of life. Christmas itself, however, comes when the days begin getting longer. Christmas is the celebration of our Light — Jesus Christ. Easter coincides with spring — new life, new growth.

The big three feasts of the church year are Christmas, Easter, and Pentecost. The church year begins with Advent, which is a season of preparation looking forward toward the end of all time and Christ's return as well as his first coming to Bethlehem. The preferred color is blue, to emphasize the hope of his coming, but many churches use purple to signify royalty.

Imagine bringing out the Easter lilies mid-way through Lent. Can you envision having Easter family gatherings before Palm Sunday? Think of celebrating a family birthday way before the event — complete with cake and ice cream. Incongruous? Of course. That is what makes Advent probably the most abused of the church year celebrations because so many of us are colored by our society which is celebrating Christmas long before the twelve days of Christmas. Christmas had its origins in a pagan holiday and that paganism remains with us not only in our celebration of Christmas, but even the various traditions such as the yule log, the Christmas tree, and reindeer.

It is easy to bypass the richness of Christmas readiness and preparation for the end times — the Parousia — because, after all, who likes thinking about such things? The word "Advent" means "coming." The first two Sundays of Advent especially point toward the end of all time — "his coming." Then "the voice of one calling in the wilderness" is heard as the third Sunday focuses on John the Baptist as the herald of Christ. The fourth Sunday centers on Mary, the mother of our Lord, as the obedient servant. Each Sunday has an important and valuable theme that is so frequently overlooked that most pastors and theologians give up on congregations actually observing Advent as Advent.

The Advent wreath symbolizes the coming of the Lord. Each lit candle further lightens our hopefulness — until Christmas — the festival of light. Christmas is not family time. It is not about turkey dinner and giving presents. Christmas is not about colorful lights and tinsel. Christmas is about God's great gift to the world — the Lord Jesus Christ — Immanuel ("God with us"). It begins at eventide December 24 and lasts just 12 short days until January 5. This is the time for

Christmas hymns and anthems, decorations and parties. Most of us, however, are so sick of Christmas music and parties by December 24 that the last thing we want to hear is more. This wonderful Lutheran heritage seems lost to contemporary, secular reality.

Then comes Epiphany! The Epiphany season serves as a bridge between Christmas (Jesus' birth) and Good Friday (his death). The season begins with the coming of the Magi (so often erroneously placed around the manger scene and confused with Christmas). The Magi represent the nations of the world. We often use this season to highlight world mission. Then we celebrate Jesus' baptism the First Sunday after the Epiphany. The Sundays until Ash Wednesday observe the various parts of Jesus' earthly ministry culminating with his Transfiguration the Sunday before Ash Wednesday. August 6 is the alternate (and traditional) date, but celebrating the Transfiguration immediately prior to Lent makes eminent sense. Jesus was transfigured just before heading to Jerusalem for his suffering and death.

White is the color of Christmas and green the color of Epiphany. But for some gold has been introduced for the day of the Epiphany, January 6, to signify the kingship and divinity of the Christ to whom the Magi offered their gifts (one of them being gold).

The Epiphany season is variable, depending upon when Easter occurs because 40 days before Easter (not counting Sundays), Ash Wednesday calls the faithful to worship and reflection on baptism and self-renewal. Many Lutheran churches have services where ashes from the palms of the previous year's Passion Sunday are placed in the sign of a cross upon the forehead of each person and they remember that they are dust and to dust they shall return. Pretty sober business! This custom, recently revived in our Lutheran Churches, has Old Testament roots where sackcloth and ashes signified repentance.

The word Lent comes from an old Anglo-Saxon word, *lencten* — originally meaning "spring." As springtime is a season for renewal and growth, so Lent is a time for discipleship and recommitment to Christian growth — beginning in the ashes of winter. Lent began as a pre-Easter fast of around 40 hours and soon stretched to include the week before Easter, then two weeks (beginning with "Passion Sunday"), and eventually, around the end of the seventh century, it was extended to the present 40 days. Forty is a significant word in the Bible: 40 days of the Flood, 40 years in the wilderness, and Jesus' own 40-day fast in the desert.

The day before Ash Wednesday, Shrove Tuesday has taken on more significance in the secular world than the religious. In England it was called Shrove Tuesday because the "shriving" (confession and absolution) of penitent believers on that day, in preparation for Lent. In France and New Orleans the day is known as *Mardi Gras* — a day of festivity and celebration. The Germans call the day *Fastnacht*. In Liberal, Kansas and Olney, England, the women have a pancake race. It is called "Fat Tuesday" and has no significance to Lutherans except as a cultural phenomena.

One Shrove Tuesday when I was a hospital chaplain, a group of us engaged in a serious theological dialogue. The discussion turned so ponderous it became somewhat boring and negative. Eventually silence enveloped our little group before one of the chaplains said, "I'll break the ice. I feel sleepy and depressed . . ." No sooner had he said the words than the fire alarm sounded. Lent had broken in to our complacency. (It happened that one of the hospital employees was burning some palm fronds in preparation for the Ash Wednesday service and that is what set off the alarm). It struck me that Ash Wednesday and the season of Lent is just such an alarm. It is a call to take seriously the peril of our lives.

Pastor Wayne Saffen framed the season well:

Lent is
Forty days till Easter,
Not counting Sundays.

Lent is actually
Six and a half weeks
Of very violet repentance
And very purple passion.

Lent is
Watching a man go to his death
And not being able to stop it.

Lent is
Helping send him
To the cross.

Lent is
Knowing this
And letting it sink in.

Lent is
Not getting off
The hook.

Lent is
Taking sin seriously,
Taking life seriously,
Taking death seriously,
Taking everything
More seriously
Than usual.

Lent is,
Among other things,
Having to wait for Spring.

Lent is
Six more weeks
Of shivering
In the cold.

Lent is
Not a very happy time,
But it is what
You have to go through
To get to Easter.[4]

(The Second Season, Wayne Saffen)

Many Lutheran churches gather for worship during the weeks of Lent, although, again, the pressure of contemporary society leave many people too tired and pressured for anything extra — like a worship service. The once well-attended mid-week Lenten services are now not so well attended — unless there is some kind of gimmick to get people out. The color is purple (although black is frequently used on Ash Wednesday).

Most Lutheran pastors will not perform marriages during Lent. Many Lutherans will "fast" in that they will give up something for Lent. Usually the discipline is not a spiritual discipline, but a health or beauty concern. There are some sincere souls who abstain from certain food, drink or activities so that their outward preparation may lead to spiritual renewal.

When a person goes on a diet, the one thing that person doesn't want to think about is food. And yet that is often the major concern of dieters. Likewise, perhaps because of the discipline of fasting, various food customs have arisen that are associated with the Lenten season. Since people often gave up meat during Lent, bread became one of the staples of Lent. Bakers even began making dough pretzels — a knotted length of dough that represented a Christian praying, with arms crossed and hands placed on opposite shoulders.

Hot cross buns are popular during Lent. The cross of course reminds the eater of Christ's cross. They are most popular on Good Friday.

The Lenten season concludes with Holy Week which begins with what most people still refer to as Palm Sunday. The *Lutheran Book Of Worship* calls it The Sunday Of The Passion. *Lutheran Worship* gives Sunday Of The Passion as an alternative. "Passion" is one of those old words easily misunderstood. When we think of passion we think of throbbing feelings of love or lust. The ancient meaning of passion is suffering. That is the emphasis on the week before Easter. The drama of our Lord's entrance into Jerusalem (complete with palms) begins this Holy Week. Many churches have a processional with palms. Then the mood quickly moves from jubilation to quiet witnessing of the events on Golgotha. The color is scarlet, the color of blood but also the color of triumph. The passion of Christ was not ultimately defeat.

Scarlet can be used throughout the week (otherwise it is violet). Scarlet must be distinguished from the bright red of Pentecost. Probably most churches do not have scarlet and will stay with the violet of Lent during Holy Week. Violet is the color of repentance as well as royalty.

Maundy Thursday (youth think it's Monday Thursday and wonder what is going on here) commemorates the Lord's Supper and our Lord's ideal of service as illustrated by his washing of the disciple's feet. The word "Maundy" (not "Maunday") comes from the Latin *mandatum* which means "command." The command is to love and serve. Footwashing would be appropriate, but happens in only a very few Lutheran services. Holy Communion is the norm at this service.

The service is solemn — often without music, the first of the Tridium — the three days. After the Maundy Thursday service the altar is stripped of all paraments. The altar, lectern and pulpit are left bare until Easter to symbolize the humiliation and barrenness of the cross.

Good Friday seems like a contradiction in terms. How can we call "good" the day associated with bad luck (Friday the 13th is supposedly the day our Lord was killed)? Of course it was not good for him and his mother and friends, but for our greater good he journeyed to the hill and hung there until it was over — "finished" he said. The work of redemption was complete, the veil in the temple was torn to illustrate the direct access we now have by the merit of Christ our Lord.

Good Friday was originally called "God's Friday." Pronunciation has changed over the years and "God be with you" has become "Goodbye" in the same way that "God's Friday" has become "Good Friday." The "Goodbye" for our Lord in his death is commemorated by placing a black veil over the cross in many of our Lutheran services.

Good Friday services are solemn. In some communities *tre ore* (three hour) services are held as a commemoration of the three hours our Lord hung on the cross. Some churches have a Tenebrae service. This service begins in a church lit by candles and gradually the candles are extinguished as Bible passages and hymns are sung. The increasing darkness illustrates the despair and loneliness of our Lord's "Goodbye." Despite the emphasis many churches put on observing the "passion" of our Lord by such services as Maundy Thursday and especially Good Friday, many prefer to avoid the messiness of the cross and jump directly into Easter joy. However something is lost when the reality of sin, darkness and suffering are glossed over as nothing important.

Easter is the essential and central festival of the church year. Without Easter there would be no Christian church. Without Easter, the faith we hold would be barren and without hope. Many of our churches begin this service with the words "Christ is risen," answered by the joyous response, "He is risen indeed!"

Easter is the most holy of our celebrations. Our faith centers around the resurrection of our Lord. This resurrection is the victory that is central to our joy. In April of 1813 Napoleon Boneparte's campaign against Austria had advanced to within six miles of the village of Feldkirch. The Austrian army was still some distance away and it looked as if Feldkirch would be occupied by the enemy Boneparte. But, as the emperor's troops advanced by night, the believers of that community gathered in the village church to pray, for it was Holy Saturday eve.

Next morning at sunrise, the bells of the church pealed out across the land announcing the resurrection. Napoleon's officers, not realizing that it was Easter Sunday, suspected that the Austrian army had moved into Feldkirch during the night and that the bells were ringing in jubilation. So the officers ordered a quick retreat and the village was saved. The bells of Easter saved the Austrian village of Feldkirch from occupation by Napoleon's troops.

The resurrection of that one man, Jesus Christ, on that first Easter outside the walls of Jerusalem signaled a new era

35

in humanity. Because he rose, all those who believe will also rise. Each Easter is an acknowledgment of that wonderful fact of our deliverance.

Easter is such a critical celebration that we set aside a week of Sundays for the Sundays *of* Easter (not Sundays *after*). For seven weeks — 50 days — the rejoicing continues until the ascension. The Paschal candle burns near the altar to signify the presence of the risen Christ. The color is white (with gold as an alternative for Easter day).

Easter culminates with the Day of Pentecost. On this 50th day the risen Lord sent the promised gift of the Comforter, the Holy Spirit. This is the day the church was born. No institution has survived as long in history as the church. Flawed by incredible human stupidity and power-grabbing, the church survives. Pressured by the society around it, the church persists in its mission. Beset by conflict, torn apart by division, the church continues proclaiming the good news of Jesus Christ. It is only by the grace of God and the power of the Holy Spirit that this church can continue doing what it has done throughout all these years. There really is no explanation.

In many Lutheran churches confirmation on Pentecost symbolizes the ongoing work of the church. Certainly the red of the paraments, banners, flowers and often the clothing of those worshiping, reminds one of the fire of Pentecost, the vigor of the Holy Spirit, and the excitement of our faith.

Pentecost is one of the big three celebrations of the church and yet, traditionally, the Lutheran churches — especially those in America — have not capitalized on its importance. Perhaps it is because we are a Christ-centered church and therefore tend to underemphasize the work of the Spirit? If this is so, maybe it is time for a change? Doesn't the Athanasian Creed (one of the three "ecumenical" creeds Lutherans espouse) say, ". . . in this Trinity, no one is before or after, greater or less than the other; but all three persons are in themselves coeternal and coequal." Perhaps there is room in our congregations for emphasizing the third person of the Trinity? Luther himself says it so eloquently in his explanation to the Third Article:

"I believe that I cannot by my own reason or strength believe in Jesus Christ, my Lord, or come to Him; but the Holy Spirit has called me ... enlightened me ... sanctified and kept me ..." The one unforgivable sin is the one against the Third Person of the Trinity. Certainly the celebration of the Holy Spirit and the birth of the church is worthy of our great efforts and determination to elevate this holy day with the other two: Christmas and Easter. This is our chance to have a truly holy day instead of a secularized merchandising occasion. The so-called Pentecostal churches do not have a monopoly on the Holy Spirit.

The Sundays *after* Pentecost represent the longest portion of the church year. Stretching from early summer to late fall, this season comprises almost half the year. The Sundays after Pentecost represent the time of the church (whereas the rest of the church year represent the life of our Lord). Both *Lutheran Worship* and the *Lutheran Book Of Worship* divide the church year into thirds: "The Time of Christmas" (*LW*), "The Time of Easter" (*LW*), and "The Time of the Church" (*LBW*). The Pentecost season has by far the largest third!

The very first Sunday after Pentecost is Trinity Sunday. We will see how critical this doctrine is in the Christian faith. Setting aside one Sunday to accentuate this doctrine's importance is the least we can do. Some congregations will use this Sunday to say the Athanasian Creed to highlight this least-used of the ecumenical creeds.

The last Sunday of the church year; the last Sunday of Pentecost, is Christ the King Sunday. On this Sunday the lordship of Jesus is the focus. As time passes and the seasons change, one thing does not change: Jesus Christ.

The church year provides us with a variety of celebrations, festivals, commemorations and occasions. All relate to and explain the faith we profess. The church year is a wonderful tool for giving us a clear picture of our Lord.

Liturgical Colors

When I was a child I appreciated the changing colors of

my Lutheran church. I enjoyed the visual splendor of the deep color in the silk paraments and wondered why they changed the colors every so often. Later I learned the significance of the colors:

White is the color of the Godhead symbolizing perfection, joy, and purity. The glorified Christ, eternity, and the holy angels suggest white.

Red is the color of blood, martyrdom, as well as fervor, and fire. It is also suggestive of love and the victorious truth of Christian teaching based on the blood of Christ.

Green is the color of growth — life. It is the dominant color of nature and is suggestive of our enlargement in the faith.

Violet is the color of mourning and repentance as well as royalty.

Blue is the color of hope and anticipation.

Black is the absence of color, symbolizing death.

Chapter Two

Brief Order For Confession And Forgiveness

Invocation

Our Lutheran service begins with the Invocation: **In the name of the Father, and of the Son, and of the Holy Spirit.**

My name is Dennis. I guess my parents liked the sound of the name. Like most American parents they gave no thought to the name's meaning. "Dennis" comes from the Greek god Dionysus, the god of wine and debauchery! That's not an exalted name! Furthermore, born about the same time as I to a cartoonist named Hank Ketchum, another Dennis would ensure that future generations not name their sons "Dennis." "Dennis the Menace" has permanently dated all of us with this appellation.

We name our children primarily because we like the sound of the name. Sometimes a name is given in order to honor someone in the family (living or dead). Occasionally the name is based on a popular song or individual. Seldom do we base names on their meaning.

What does your name mean? Probably half of us have no idea. Even fewer see any significance in our names. That was not the case in biblical times. The ancient Jews gave their children names, not because they liked the sound, but because of the special meaning. "Jesus," for example, means "Savior." "Christ" means "Messiah — the anointed one." "Emmanuel" comes from two words: *Emmanu*, which means "with us," and *El*, "God."

Names not only identified one person as distinct from another (such as we use them in our day), but they also expressed the essential nature of the person as well. One could tell another's character by that person's name. When Abigail excuses her husband, she does so on the basis of his name: "My Lord, do not take seriously this ill-natured fellow, Nabal; for as his name is, so is he; Nabal is his name, and folly is with him." (1 Samuel 25:25) "Nabal" in Hebrew means "fool." If a person's character changes, so then does that person's name. When the patriarch Jacob was born, he was named such because Jacob means "He takes by the heel," which is exactly what happened when Jacob was born — he had his brother's heel in his hand at birth. This definition of his character carries forth in his subsequent behavior with his older brother. He takes his brother by the heel again as he outmaneuvers him to obtain the birthright. When Jacob wrestled with God and became the forebear of a great nation, his name was changed to "Israel," — which means "The one who strives with God."

The temple in Jerusalem was built for God's name! Here is where God chose to reveal God's name and have that name dwell. God lives in heaven, but God's presence, as symbolized by the name, resides in Jerusalem. When Jesus came, he came in the name of God. Today we pray in the name of Jesus. We baptize in the name of the Lord. We begin our worship with that "name which is above every name."

The Jews reasoned that names gave a person special power over another. To know one's name meant to have a special relationship with that person and to have some degree of control over him or her. When Jesus cast out demons, he asked them their names. In ancient times a window in the church was opened so that demons might flee the church at the invocation of that sacred name.

The word *Invocation* is a Latin word meaning, "to call upon." The dictionary defines Invocation as the act of calling upon — in our case — God. We begin our Christian lives calling upon God to be our God. These are the words Jesus instructed his disciples to use in baptizing the world. These are beginning words. Beginning our life-long Christian journey; beginning our worship service.

In the Invocation we *call upon* God to be present; to be near us. The truth is God is already present; God is already near. These words remind us of God's near presence.

Father

We begin in the name of the Father, Son, and Holy Spirit. What does this mean?

The word Father can convey a mixed message. A seminarian, teaching a catechism class, got quite upset with a boy who was deaf and refused to have anything to do with the first article of the Creed. "No! God is not like that!" he enthusiastically signed.

The seminarian went to his supervisory pastor and explained his frustration with the class and this boy in particular. He innocently asked, "What's the big deal about the First Article?"

"You're asking the wrong person," the pastor said. "You need to find out from the boy. You see this boy's parents are divorced and on the weekends his father gets custody. His father has been known to beat his son for being deaf. The word 'father' has bad connotations for this young man."

But we use the word Father as a description of God the Creator. In some ways use of the word "Mother" would be even more appropriate (except we have no direct scriptural

41

examples where God is called "Mother"). There are, however, Old Testament references to God as being like a mother:

> *Listen to me, O house of Jacob, all the remnant of the house of Israel, who have been borne by me from your birth, carried from the womb; . . . I have made, and I will bear; I will carry and will save.*
>
> (Isaiah 46:3-4)
>
> *Can a woman forget her nursing child, or show no compassion for the child of her womb? Even these may forget, yet I will not forget you.*
>
> (Isaiah 49:15)

I had one woman who came to me very upset. "Pastor," she said, "They told us at the conference that God is not a man!" She went on to explain that we all know God is a man. "It says that God is our 'Father' in the Bible." Despite all my expounding, she could not, would not accept the fact that God is sexless. God is Spirit — neither male nor female.

We will talk about the male image of God later. What is important here is that in this brief phrase called the "Invocation" we have a summary of what we know about God. The first word, "Father," is telling us that God is Creator. Everything that is came from God the Creator.

The creation is the most common argument for the existence of God. It is called the argument from design. Surely, if there is an object, there had to be a designer and builder of that object. This reflects the human experience that nothing we make is made by chance. Everything comes about by design.

Edith Sitwell describes the argument best: "Seeing the immense design of the world, one image of wonder mirrored by another image of wonder — the pattern of fern and of feather echoed by the frost on the window pane, the six rays of the snowflake mirrored by the rock crystal's six-rayed eternity — I ask myself, 'Were those shapes molded by blindness? Who, then, shall teach me doubt?' "

So in this Invocation we invoke the presence of the Maker of it all: God the Creator. That itself is awesome! Creation is awesome and its maker even more so. However, if God were only Creator, that would not concern us except that the Maker's presence would so overpower and frighten us that we could not stand to invoke that Presence. But we know God has another side as well. A side not proven, but important. I'm talking, of course, about God's love.

The *New York Times* had a story about Meg Hodgkin Lippert, an educational consultant and professional storyteller who was conducting a workshop called, "Family Folklore: Preserving the Stories of the Past."

At this workshop, a small, middle-aged woman stood and began speaking somewhat nervously. She explained that she was born in Estonia. "And I have never told anyone this story until now." She looked about hesitantly before she began describing how, when she was a child, her parents had given her a beautiful doll. "It was from France," the woman explained. "I named her Che'rie. It was my most precious possession."

Then when she was 12 her cousin Doris came to stay with her. Doris' father had died and she needed a place to stay. Doris also loved Che'rie and played with her constantly. And when it was time to leave, she clutched Che'rie to her bosom. "Doris has lost her father, and she needs the doll more than you do," the 12-year-old's mother explained. "Let Doris have it. God will return it to you."

"I cried and cried," the woman said. "As time passed and Che'rie was not returned, I quit believing in God." This was a harrowing time. "This was when we had to flee Estonia because of the Nazis," she said. Over time she learned that Doris's house had been bombed and totally destroyed by the Luftwaffe. Doris, however, had escaped the burning house with only the clothes on her back. Before long all the relatives had fled Estonia. Those not killed were dispersed to the four corners of the earth in new lands.

The woman eventually settled in the United States. The years went by but they did not fade her memory of Che'rie, that priceless, lost doll. Years later she was surprised to learn that Doris was still alive and living in the United States. Their paths crossed several times, but no mention was ever made of the doll.

"When my first child was born," she said, "Doris came to visit. She brought with her a present." The woman struggled with tears. "It was Che'rie," she said. "Doris told me that when she ran from the burning house, she put Che'rie in her kerchief. She carried Che'rie all through the war.

"If you think I wept before," the woman continued, "it was nothing to the tears I wept when I saw Che'rie. And then my faith in God was restored. For what my mother had said was true."

God's other side is the gentle, loving lover of human beings like you and like me. God is a God of lovely dolls like Che'rie. God is a God of tender giving and receiving such as exemplified by Doris. And that brings us to the fullest expression of this side of God: Jesus Christ.

Son

The word Son sums up the life, ministry, death and resurrection of Jesus Christ. The Son is the "alpha and the omega" — the first and the last. It is appropriate that the service begins as alpha begins the Greek alphabet. In baptism we begin our Christian journey by joining the death and resurrection of the Son — Jesus Christ. Our baptism is a time when we receive our "Christening" — our "Christian" names.

The Son is the revealing of God's love. The Creator could have been content to create, stand back, and let creation take its course. But we believe God loves this creation — especially those created in God's image.

How does this creating God communicate love? Perhaps an option would be for God to stand in the clouds and shout to the people, "Don't be afraid, I love you!" We would be terrified! An alternative: God could make love conditional: "Do this and I'll love you ... Do that and I'll condemn you forever ...?" God certainly has that right. But conditional love is not really love is it? Another option is that God could force us to love. Such force would violate our free will and make us into automatons who have no option but to love our Creator God.

God had good news to communicate (*good news* is the meaning of "Gospel") and the way God did it was through the Son, Jesus Christ. The incarnation.

It was Christmas eve and the old skeptic wanted to just go to bed and forget all that Christmas eve "Hocus-pocus" as he called it. "You try to tell me that God became a baby?" he once asked a visiting minister. "That's ridiculous. First of all, if there is a God, why should that God be interested in us human beings? Secondly, why would God trouble himself to become one of us. This just doesn't make sense to me. Count me out of your religious stuff," he concluded.

This particular Christmas eve was bitterly cold and the snow was falling heavier by the hour. As the old man rested before his cozy fireplace thinking about turning in for the night, he thought of the many animals that would suffer and perhaps die in the cold darkness. As he thought about it, he wondered, "I wish I could save some of them — the birds especially. I wish I could invite them into my warm sanctuary and have them stay for the night."

As he thought about the cold birds, he slipped off into a slumber before his fireplace. And he dreamed. He dreamed that he opened his door to the birds, but they wouldn't come in. They were freezing in the snow. They would die by morning but they would not come in.

"They don't trust me," he said. "They don't trust me ... The only way they could trust me is if I could earn their trust some how or another." And in his dream that is exactly what happened. He earned the trust of the animals by becoming a bird and flying into the storm and living among them. He had a message for the others: "Trust that man! We can spend the night in the warmth of that cabin. It's better than freezing to death and is actually quite pleasant. He's got food for us to eat and water to drink and roosts to rest our weary bodies. Come," he said to his fellow birds, "let's go."

At that point the man woke up. "Why that's it! The birds are like us human beings. By nature we are afraid of God. God became one of us so that we might learn to trust!" For the first time, the incarnation made sense.

When Jesus became one of our kind, we rejected him and hung him on a cross to die. Why? Human nature. People like to win and they like winners. The Jews in Jesus' day were no different from you and me. For centuries they had been losers. They had lost sovereignty to Greece and then to Rome. They had lost their unity. They had lost wars and attempts to overthrow their overlords. But then along came a rabbi with great promise. His name was "Jesus" — a name which means "Savior." His career grew and the groundswell of public support reached a flood stage. As Jesus headed for Jerusalem, the Jews had visions of his claiming the throne of Israel with the crown of David on his head. They saw the hated Roman invaders routed, running in retreat from their holy land. Though greatly inferior to the Roman military might, they had God on their side and God would prevail. It was God who had rescued them from the powerful Egyptians many years before. Surely God would aid their cause — God's cause — now.

What a shock the words of Jesus must have been to the expectant people! He turned to the jubilant crowd and talked of hating loved ones and loving hated ones; bearing one's cross and giving everything up for the kingdom of God; forgiving wrongs done to us as God forgives our wrongs. But they (and we) did not want to hear about such things. They (and we) wanted to hear about getting — not giving; winning — not losing; living — not dying; justice — not forgiveness. They wanted to hear about crowns worn, not crosses borne. And so do we!

The cross was the stumbling block. It kept many from believing. It still does. But to those who believe, it is the very symbol of salvation.

From the earliest days of Christianity, Christians have marked the sign of the cross on their bodies. It reminded them of God's love; God's mercy; God's efforts to reach us through the blizzard of human sin and depravity. It reminded them of God's "Word made flesh" — the word that effectively communicated unlike any other word. Writing in A.D. 200, Tertullian says, "In all our undertakings — when we enter a place or leave it; before we dress; before we bathe; when we take our meals; when we light the lamps in the evening; before we retire at night; when we sit down to read; before each new task — we trace the sign of the cross on our foreheads."

The sign of the cross is made when one is baptized. ". . . Child of God, you have been sealed by the Holy Spirit and marked with the cross of Christ forever." Luther instructed his followers to make the sign of the cross in remembrance of their baptisms. In the *Small Catechism*, he instructed, "In the morning, when you get up (In the evening, when you go to bed) make the sign of the holy cross and say: In the name of the Father and of the Son and of the Holy Ghost. Amen." In the *Large Catechism* he instructs parents to teach their children to cross themselves.

The sign of the cross does not have to be anything fancy. Simply made on the forehead or the breast or even on the palm of one's hand in secret. The cross helps us remember who we are and whose we are.

So when we begin our worship service with the Invocation, we begin with a short description of God as well as actions that describe in brief, what God has done for us — on the cross. Words plus action. God's presence plus our mindfulness. This is the Invocation.

Holy Spirit

God is the Creator. That's understandable. It seems

reasonable that Someone had to make it all. We have God the Son. The loving side of God makes sense in Jesus. Jesus was like you and me — fully human. He ate, drank, walked, talked, suffered and died. Jesus is the human side of God — the comprehensible side. Jesus is the "Word made Flesh" as John puts it. But what about the Holy Spirit?

Luther, in his *Small Catechism* explains the third article like this:

> *I believe that I cannot by my own reason or strength believe in Jesus Christ, my Lord, or come to him; but the Holy Ghost has called me by the Gospel, enlightened me with His gifts, sanctified and kept in the true faith, even as He calls, gathers, enlightens, and sanctifies the whole Christian Church ...*

In other words, without the Holy Spirit, the whole enterprise would be lost. I cannot decide to believe in God. The initiative rests solely with God. I don't like this. This is hard for me to follow. After all, I "make a decision" to believe in Christ, don't I? Don't I have something to do with faith? Don't I have the initiative? As they say, "If it is to be it's up to me."

Dennis Kastens tells the story of the old days when the West was being settled. It seems a young man, who had never done anything very wrong, one day lost his temper playing cards. Picking up a revolver, he shot his opponent and killed him. The man was arrested, tried, and sentenced to hang. But because of the good life he had previously lived, his relatives and friends got up a petition for his defense. It seemed as though everyone wanted to sign it. Before long other towns and communities heard about it, and people all over the state eagerly signed the petition.

Finally it was taken to the governor who was overwhelmed at the large baskets filled with petitions. He decided to pardon the young man, and so, writing out the pardon, he put it in his pocket, and then, dressed in the attire of a clergyman, he made his way to the prison. (Why he did this, I don't know). As he approached the death cell, the young man sprang to the bars. "Get out of here, I don't want to see you. They have offered chaplains to me seven times already and each time I have refused." "But," said the governor, "wait a moment. I have something for you. Let me talk to you." "Listen, if you don't get out of here at once, I'll call the guard and have you put out," said the young man. "But," exclaimed the governor, "I have news for you, the very best. Won't you let me tell you about it?" "You heard what I said," responded the young man, "and if you don't leave immediately, I'll call the warden." "Very well," replied the governor, and with a sad heart he turned and left.

In a few moments the warden approached. "Well young man, I see you had a visit from the governor." "What! Was that man dressed in the garb of a clergyman the governor?" "He was, and he had a pardon in his pocket for you but you wouldn't even listen to him."

"Get me a pen, get me ink, get me paper," cried the young man. And sitting down he wrote:

"Dear Governor: I owe you an apology. I am sorry for the way I treated you ..." The governor received the letter, turned it over and wrote on the back, "No longer interested in this case." The day came for the young man to be executed. "Is there anything you want to say before you die?" the executioner asked. "Yes," said the young man. "Tell the young men of America that I am not dying for my crime. I am not dying because I am a murderer. The governor pardoned me. I could have lived. Tell them that I am dying because I would not listen to the governor's offer." And with that he was executed.

Whether the story is true, an embellishment of a story, or just a story, the lesson applies: We come to God by means of the Holy Spirit. And, while the Holy Spirit is powerful, God respects our free will. We have the power to say "NO!" to God.

Jesus called this saying "No!" to God the "unforgivable sin." It is unforgivable because it cuts a person from the very source of grace and forgiveness.

Many churches have paintings or stained glass windows showing Jesus standing outside a door knocking. Most of the representations also show the door as having no latch. The implication is that the door is opened only from the inside. So it is that God gently knocks at the doors of our lives. We have the freedom to leave the door closed or open it and receive the wonderful, powerful, light of God's grace.

The same is true for the worship service. In the Invocation we invite God to be present. God is already present, knocking at the door of our lives. God is present on Sunday morning or whenever the service is held. God seeks entry into the holy of holies — our lives. "Behold I stand at the door and knock," says Jesus. The Invocation is the *beginning* of our relationship with God by the waters of Holy Baptism. The Invocation is the *continuing* of our relationship with God by the spirit of the worship service. Have an open heart and open mind to the very Spirit of God — the Holy Spirit, present in this place at this time — for you!

The Confession

"I could never belong to a church that started out with a confession of sins," the college professor said. "Who wants to begin with garbage? My philosophy is, forget the bad stuff and move on!"

Easily said, but not so easily done. Most people carry a great deal of "bad stuff" around with them from day to day. Guilt is a pervasive element of modern life. One can bury guilt (like the college professor suggested), work to repay one's sin, or receive forgiveness.

When guilt is overlooked and we attempt to bury it, it refuses to remain buried. Like ghosts coming from the tombs, guilt rises as a spectral shadow haunting the background of one's life. It's that basic, uneasy feeling people have in living from day to day. It's the feeling that says, "You're no good" or "You're not as good as some people . . ." Guilt hangs in the shadows accusing us of not being what we should be; not living up to our standards; not doing what is right; doing what is wrong. Guilt, simply defined, is the gap between what we know is right and the reality of our living. That gap appears in every human life because no one is perfect.

The confession helps us clear the air. The confession helps us get the gap in our actions on the table — in the open. Hiding it; denying it is destructive to human life.

Perhaps no one knows this better than persons in recovery. Alcoholism, for example, is tremendously destructive. Denial that there is a problem is part of the problem. I myself have counseled alcoholics who have lost their jobs, their spouses and families, their homes, their health — everything because of their drinking — and yet they deny they have a drinking problem. "I can stop if I want to," they tell me. "Why not stop now?" "Okay" they say. But I know from years of experience that will not happen. The only way an alcoholic can stop drinking is to become honest with himself and admit he has no control over the gap between his intentions and his actions.

The first and critical step of Alcoholics Anonymous is: "We admitted we were powerless over alcohol — that our lives had become unmanageable." The first and critical step of the Christian church is: "We confess . . ."

To hide the fact of our bondage to sin only destroys us. Confession enlivens us; makes us human; gives us power to change and improve. Confession is our reality check time. Confession is powerful.

Stubborn human nature does not like to admit openly to shortcomings, faults, or sin. We prefer dealing with our guilt in other ways. Many do seek to deny it and are content to leave it in the background of their daily living. This is perhaps the most prevalent means of guilt disposal. But another way to deal with guilt (the gap between intention and reality) is to earn our way out of guilt.

One young man had a terrible temper. One day he was in a heated argument with a friend and his temper flared beyond the boiling point. He struck the friend with his fist and hit him on the side of the head, knocking him down. In the end, this friend lost the eye on that side of his head. The quick-tempered young man immediately felt immense remorse. He thought about his actions. He felt terrible. The guilt grew with passing time. He recalled Jesus' words about "If your hand causes you to sin, cut it off." (Matthew 5:30)

With iron-willed determination — driven by raw guilt — this young man went to the furnace on a winter day, opened the door and held the hand that struck the blow over the fire until it was burned useless for life. He did it! He had won release from his guilt by punishing himself. But at what cost? Who did he help? What good did this repayment do? This story is true and, even though the details are different, this same sad story repeats itself every time one tries to repay the guilt by self-punishment.

Burying and denying the guilt or punishing oneself are two ways of dealing with what we in the church call sin: the gap between knowing and doing what is right. The third option is confession. Confession can be done as a group (corporate) such as in the liturgy or it can be individual. In the Lutheran Church confession is important. It has been suggested that we must never think we understand any of Luther's thought until we have reduced it to the simple idea of the forgiveness of sins through Jesus Christ. This thought was the dominant idea in the many writings of Martin Luther.

That being so, it is interesting that corporate confession was not practiced in the early days of the Lutheran Church. In Luther's liturgies, for example, all references to the confession were omitted. There was not much historical precedent for the confession. Throughout the early days of the entire Christian church there was no confession as part of the service. The *Didache*, an early Christian document, admonishes Christians to "Assemble on the day of the Lord, break bread and celebrate the Eucharist; but first confess your sins, that your sacrifice may be holy." But this confession was private, not corporate.

Confession was seen by the reformers as a preparatory rite. This is why it is put before the regular liturgy in Lutheran services. It is a preparatory and an optional (although popular) part of the service.

So far we have been talking about Confession, but that is not all that is involved. The title in the *Lutheran Book Of Worship* is *Brief Order For Confession And Forgiveness* (*Lutheran Worship* calls this part simply *The Preparation*). Confession is one part. When Judas Iscariot betrayed Jesus, he felt guilt. He confessed his sin. And then he punished himself for his sin (option number two) by committing suicide. Confession, as good as it is, is only part of the story. The entire story includes forgiveness. Peter confessed his sin in betraying Jesus, but he also received forgiveness. That subtle distinction made Peter a saint and Judas a devil; it created life for Peter and death for Judas. And that same distinction remains for us today. Confession is not complete without forgiveness (also call Absolution).

Forgiveness sounds easy — and it is! It is passive. It is like receiving a present because it is a present — the most beautiful of all presents. But for most of us, forgiveness does not come easily. Why? Because it means receiving something for nothing. It means not being punished as we deserve. It means being dependent.

The natural human inclination is to earn forgiveness as we have to earn everything else in life. But, as we have discussed, this cannot be done without great cost. Our only option is to passively receive the gift of grace.

John Newton, an English sailor, had accumulated quite large sums of money by bringing human beings to England from Africa and selling them as slaves. But his conscience got to him. He turned to alcohol (option number one in dealing with guilt) and self-hatred. One night in London he passed by a small mission hall where someone was preaching. He stepped inside to listen and was challenged by the message that Christ died for the sins of all people — no matter how great. He opened his life to God that night by receiving forgiveness. Not only did his life change as he realized that his sins were forgiven, he dedicated his life to bringing hope and freedom to others as well. If God could save a wretch like him, who had enslaved people, then surely there was something John Newton could do to show his appreciation. One expression was a hymn that has moved millions of people: *Amazing Grace.*

> *Amazing grace, how sweet the sound,*
> *That saved a wretch like me!*
> *I once was lost, but now am found;*
> *Was blind, but now I see.*

Receiving Absolution — forgiveness is powerful stuff. It is life-changing. Gratitude to the living God of grace is one of the great emotions true absolution generates. That wonderful grace is free and undeserved, but it usually has a marvelous effect because of what it does to the human heart. Hearts overflowing with gratitude often prompt recovering sinners to go forth in joyful, thankful and loving service to God and others.

Forgiveness, while free and undeserved, does obligate us to forgive others who have hurt us. Through the words of scripture Jesus asks us about a debtor who owed a huge sum and is forgiven by a gracious king. When this forgiven debtor turns to someone who owes him a small sum and threatens him with debtor's prison "until he would pay the debt," the gracious king asks, "Should you not have had mercy on your fellow slave, as I had mercy on you?" And the parable concludes: "So my heavenly Father will also do to every one of you, if you do not forgive your brother or sister from your heart." (Matthew 18:23-35) When Jesus shows mercy on a woman of ill repute, he asks which forgiven creditor will love the master more, the one forgiven 500 dennarii or the one forgiven 50? On the spot Jesus forgives the woman and evokes a scandal. "The one to whom little is forgiven, loves little," he tells his followers. In his great prayer Jesus taught that we are to forgive those who trespass against us as we have been forgiven our trespasses. Another version of that wonderful prayer says that we forgive the debt owed us as we have had our debt cancelled. In other words, we are "even" (as in "getting even" — vengeance, justice, right making right).

The Brief Order For Confession And Forgiveness or The Preparation ends with the declaration of our forgiveness by God and self, but this is just the beginning of our obligation to forgive. If the service stopped right here and went no further and if every Lutheran worshiping every Sunday could or would take to heart the implications of this part of the service, the world would see an incredible force for good and the grace of God.

Sir Walter Scott was once bothered by a stray dog. Picking up a stone, he threw it at the dog, intending to frighten it. But he had thrown the stone harder and straighter than planned, and hit the dog in the foreleg, breaking it badly. Instead of becoming vicious or running away, the dog limped to Sir Walter Scott's side and licked his hand — the very hand that had thrown the stone.

Such is to be our forgiveness of ourselves and others. As Confession is facing up to the reality of our shortfalls, Forgiveness is facing up to the reality of other's shortfalls with us and our own failures to live up to the highest of standards. Forgiveness means sustaining all the hurt and injury of the past and accepting the person who did it. It means loving the person who committed the injury. Like the dog who had been injured, the forgiven person responds in grace.

Easy? Not on your life! This is perhaps the most difficult thing a person can do. That is why forgiveness is so seldom practiced. It is hard — one of the hardest things to accomplish. Living a forgiving lifestyle is surely one of the greatest challenges facing every individual Christian. Sometimes the hurts are so tremendously deep; sometimes the pain is so severe that forgiveness comes only with great difficulty.

Watching the news, one can see how difficult forgiveness is. There are always wars going on somewhere on the planet. One group has been hurt and retaliates against another. The cycle of violence escalates until one side is defeated and the other "victorious." By the end of the war precious human lives have been lost, millions upon millions has been spent, and usually the hatred continues unabated until the next opportunity for its expression in more bloodshed. Surely the most effective way to break the cycle is unconditional forgiveness — as God forgives us!

The confession concludes with the declaration of forgiveness spoken by the pastor. This declaration comes in several forms: the declarative form — "I therefore declare to you the entire forgiveness of all your sins." This form of forgiveness is based on the Office of the Keys which takes Christ's words that who-so-ever's sins you forgive, they are forgiven. (John 20:23) When the minister says "I declare to you the entire forgiveness of all your sins," the pastor is not doing so *personally*. The minister is speaking for Christ.

Sometimes this becomes even more dramatic when the pastor says, "I . . . forgive you all your sins." This takes Christ's Office of the keys to a more personal level. This is the approach often used by pastors in cases of individual confession and forgiveness.

The third form might be called the prayer form of absolution. "In the mercy of almighty God, Jesus Christ was given to die for you, and for his sake God forgives you all your sins."

That's all there is to Confession and Forgiveness. That's all — but what an "all" it is! Freedom itself is given! The obligation to forgive as we have been forgiven has been pronounced! If we could take this part of the service alone and follow it, the world would be a tremendously better place for all — Christian and non-Christian alike! There, again, is that gap between what we should do and what we do or don't do! God forgive us! Amen.

Chapter Three

Now we get to the service. Up to this point we have been preparing for the service. One of the first things we notice in our Lutheran services is numbered red lettering. These are called *rubrics* which is a Latin word meaning red. In ancient times instructions for worship were written in red and the text in black. The *Lutheran Book Of Worship* and *Lutheran Worship* do the same today. The *rubrics* give us instruction.

In *Lutheran Worship rubric number one says: "A hymn of invocation MAY be sung."* The *rubric* in the *Lutheran Book Of Worship* says *"The Brief Order for Confession and Forgiveness ... MAY be used before this service."* I have deliberately emphasized the word *"MAY"* in both worship books because one of the things we learn about *rubrics* is to watch the verbs "may" and "is." "May" means exactly that: we may choose to use this or we may not wish to. Neither worship book employ any "shall" *rubrics* (although that is what they are whenever the word MAY is absent).

The first *rubric* in the *Lutheran Book Of Worship* confirms what was said above: the confession is a preparatory part of the service. It is a PRE-service. It can be done at home or before the prelude or the hymn or not at all.

Rubric number two in *The Lutheran Book Of Worship* says *"The minister MAY announce the day and its significance before the Entrance Hymn, before the lessons, or at another appropriate time."*

The purpose of such an announcement is to clearly articulate the theme of the day. Each Lutheran service has a theme — a central point — that the hymns, the lessons, the Prayer of the Day, and the sermon revolve around.

Rubric number three says: *"When there is no Communion, the service is concluded after the Creed as indicated."*

Okay, so we know that. Most Lutherans still don't have Holy Communion each Sunday. Most Lutheran services, like it or not, still abbreviate the service and make it essentially a service of the Word.

Stand. The rubric simply says stand.

No "MAY" *rubric* here!

Many non-Lutherans feel that a Lutheran service is an exercise in exercise because of all the standing and sitting, standing and sitting. We begin with standing for the Hymn Of Invocation or Entrance Hymn. Standing is a way of showing our respect for God. When addressing God or hearing the Gospel read, we stand. In the case of the Entrance Hymn, however, we stand not only for respect but so that it's not just the pastor and assisting minister who are standing as they enter the worship space. We are all in this together.

Entrance Hymn or Hymn Of Invocation

The Hymn begins most Lutheran services. This hymn sets the tone of the day. It should articulate the theme that will be carried throughout the whole service. Few people realize what a challenge it is to find a hymn that will vocalize the theme set forth in the texts of the day. Finding the appropriate words may not be that difficult, but finding a text that the congregation can easily sing often presents the biggest obstacle. The words can be ever-so-perfect, but if the congregation stumbles through a hymn that even the musically-gifted would struggle through, the tone of the service is set and it is set negatively. When a hymn is used at the very beginning of the service, it is supremely important because it does help set the theme and certainly establishes the atmosphere of the entire service.

Greeting (LBW)

The minister greets the congregation with the words common to the apostle Paul. It is called the "Apostolic Greeting" because it comes from the apostles. This is the first of four similar greetings in the service. Here is where the minister wishes for grace ... love ... and communion. Then before the Prayer of the Day comes the "salutation" where the minister says simply, **"The Lord be with you,"** and the congregation says, **"And also with you."** The third such interchange comes after the service of the word and before the service of the sacrament — the Peace. Here the minister wishes the congregation, **"The peace of the Lord be with you always."** And they say again, **"And also with you."** The final salutation comes as part of The Great Thanksgiving where the minister says again, **"The Lord be with you."**

Three key words greet the congregation in this first interchange: Grace ... Love ... Communion of "our Lord Jesus Christ ... God ... and ... the Holy Spirit." Here again we come back to the Trinity. An attribute of each person of the Trinity is named. The Pastor wishes this grace, love and communion upon the congregation, and the congregation responds with **"And also with you."**

Love we can understand. Communion we will discuss later. But what about this thing called "grace?" In the hallway of the courthouse a mother caught the judge presiding over the case of her only son. "Please, sir," she said, "have mercy." "But," said the judge, "he does not deserve mercy." "Sir," the mother responded, "It would not be mercy if he deserved it." Grace is mercy undeserved.

59

Perhaps another way of describing the difference between justice, mercy, and grace is something that might have happened to you as a child. You did something wrong. You knew it was wrong. Perhaps your mother spanked your bottom for what you did. That would be *justice*.

After you have received the punishment, your mother says, "Dear, I love you and you know you deserve more than a spanking, but I am only going to send you to your room." That is *mercy*. *Mercy* — compassionate treatment.

Grace goes beyond mercy. *Grace* is when that loving mother of yours takes you down to the local ice-cream store and buys you your favorite flavor of ice-cream — double dipped! — even though you did wrong!

Again, John Newton said it so well:

> *"Amazing grace, how sweet the sound that saved a wretch like me."*

John Newton, recovering sinner by the grace of the living God, had this inscribed on his tombstone:

JOHN NEWTON
CLERK
ONCE AN INFIDEL AND LIBERTINE
A SERVANT OF SLAVES IN AFRICA
WAS
BY THE RICH MERCY OF OUR LORD
AND SAVIOR JESUS CHRIST
PRESERVED, RESTORED, PARDONED,
AND APPOINTED TO PREACH
THE FAITH HE HAD LONG
LABORED TO DESTROY

Grace is truly "amazing!"

Why is it so hard for us to accept that amazing grace? Why do we constantly try to earn it? What keeps us from calmly reaching out and receiving the free gift and living lives of freedom and peace?

Perhaps it is because we all know "You can't get something for nothing." Everything has a price tag. We know all about economy. We understand that to get you have to give. Nothing is for nothing!

Grace goes against all this common sense. Grace takes a newborn child — helpless, unable to make deals, unknowing about anything spiritual — and makes that child one of God's own. Grace takes a death-row killer who mutilated and tortured his last victim and turns him into a "saint." Grace takes the 95-year-old infidel, who, despite leading a life of ridicule of Christianity, on her death-bed confesses Jesus as Lord. Is grace fair? Absolutely not! Otherwise it would be called "justice" and not "grace." Is grace merciful? Absolutely! But it is mercy carried to the extreme.

A very active lay woman died and went to the Pearly Gates of heaven. "And why should I let you in," Peter inquired. "What have you to show for heaven? You need 1,000 points."

"Well," the woman replied, "I attended church faithfully for more than 60 years."

"Wonderful!" Peter replied. "That's two points."

"I tithed 10 percent of my income and even went beyond the tithe in my giving," she continued.

"Good. That's another two points. You certainly had your priorities straight."

"Well," the woman stumbled, "I never cheated anyone. I never lied. I never stole anything. I always told the truth and tried to treat everyone of all races and nationalities with love and respect."

"We need more like you," Peter said. "That's worth three points."

The woman figured in her head, "Two plus two plus three is only seven points," she said to Peter. "Why I'll never get in heaven except by the grace of God."

"That's 993 points! Welcome home daughter," the smiling saint said as he embraced the newest entrant in that divine kingdom.

Free and undeserved. That's grace. Motivated by the mercy and love of God; earned by Jesus Christ on the cross; conveyed by the power of the Holy Spirit, that's grace!

The grace of God is the very heart and soul of Lutheranism. It was God's grace that gave power to the Reformation movement. The church at the time was in bondage to the law: "Do this . . . and this . . . and this . . . and you might be saved." Do greater works to find a greater place in purgatory and get to heaven sooner.

Since the human tendency is to keep on trying harder and harder to save self, the church is in continual reformation. That is why Reformation Sunday in the Lutheran Church is a vital celebration of grace and needs to bring us back again and again to this central concept of our faith.

Kyrie (LW and LBW)

When I was a child, one evening before Christmas, we drove around town looking at the Christmas lights. Our family did this every year. This time, however, I was with my cousins and aunt and uncle. I remember one doorway was decorated: 'MERRY X-MAS.' I asked my aunt and uncle what that means.

"People are always trying to make Christmas a secular holiday," my aunt replied. "Instead of saying 'Christ' they say 'X.' They are trying to 'X' out the name of our Lord."

Ten years later I would be using "X" as I took notes in religion classes to denote "Christ." I was not "X-ing" the name of my Lord. I had learned in college Greek class that "X" is the Greek letter for our English "Chi" and is the first letter to the Greek spelling of "Christ."

College Greek also explained to me other symbols I frequently saw in Lutheran churches: "XP" (often superimposed) stand for "CHR" of "CHRist." IHS does not stand for "Israel High School" as one of my confirmation classmates told me. It stands for "JES" of "JESus." That A and the horseshoe are really an Alpha and an Omega — the first and last letters of the Greek alphabet (symbolizing that Christ is the first and the last of all creation as it says in the book of Revelation).

Kyrie is a Greek remnant still in our liturgy. The word is a Greek word. Greek is the language of the New Testament. Jesus spoke Aramaic, a form of Hebrew, but the New Testament books, so far as scholars can determine, were written in Greek — which was the world language of the day — much as English is today.

The Kyrie is an ancient element of our liturgy probably adapted from pagan worship. (Lest that offend you, it might be well to remember that many things from paganism were incorporated into our Christian faith such as Christmas, Epiphany, even the word "Easter" comes from the Old English word *Eastre* which means "dawn goddess" or "goddess of spring.")

The word Kyrie literally means "Lord" and comes from the phrase used in pagan and perhaps ancient Jewish worship "Lord have mercy." The entire Greek phrase, used in some modern liturgies, is Kyrie Eleison.

Rubric number six in the *LBW* says *"The Kyrie may follow." Rubric number four* in *LW* says *"The Kyrie is sung. Hymn 209, 'Kyrie, God Father,' may be used as an alternate."*

The Kyrie may or may not be used according to *Lutheran Book Of Worship* practice. It is more often used during seasons of the church year that do not have green as the color. In other words, the seasons of Epiphany and Pentecost — which constitute half the year — "may" not have the Kyrie. *Lutheran Worship* makes the Kyrie a "shall" rubric.

Two words stand out in the *LBW* Kyrie: Peace and, of course, Mercy. The word Peace is used three times (plus again in the Hymn of Praise that immediately follows) and Mercy is used four times in this brief litany. Both words, in contemporary usage, are negative. Peace means "the absence of conflict." Mercy means "refraining from harm." We will talk about the concept of Peace later. For now let's look at the meaning of Mercy.

When I think of mercy, I think of things like "mercy killing" which is a killing of someone in pain. We use another Greek word to describe mercy killing: euthanasia. The whole concept of mercy reminds me of someone in power having mercy over someone who is under that power. One definition of mercy is "a disposition to forgive or be kind." And that is a description of God.

Isaiah pictures the mercy of God as being like a loving mother. "Can a woman forget her nursing child, or show no compassion for the child of her womb? Even these may forget, yet I will not forget you," says the Lord. Our God — like a loving, doting mother. That is a good picture of mercy. That is the picture to conjure in the Kyrie. The image is one of tenderness, kindness, not wrath and sternness.

Thomas Edison, of all people, gives us a good picture of the mercy we are talking about. Francis Jahl, who was a boy with the great scientist when he invented the incandescent lamp and the phonograph, tells about an autumn day when Edison was walking in the woods bordering the laboratories. He saw something moving on the ground. It was a little wounded bird, prevented by some accident from accompanying the others of its species in their annual migration to the warmer south. The great scientist gathered the little creature in his hands, took it inside and nursed it back to health. Fearing the bird would be unable to make the long journey, Edison designed a travel residence, fitted with all known bird facilities and personally took it to the express office where he mailed it to an address in South America, where the birds migrated. That is an example of mercy — kindness in action.

The Kyrie is not a plea to God to forgive us — that's been done! We're not repeating the confession here. The Kyrie is a reminder of God's infinite kindness to us, the world, and the Church of God. The Kyrie is a plea that God's tender mercy would especially be in "this holy house, and for all who offer here their worship and praise."

Throughout the Old Testament especially we hear that God is "merciful and gracious, slow to anger, and abounding in steadfast love." (Genesis 34:6, Nehemiah 9:17, Psalm 86:15, 103:8; 145:8, Joel 2:13, Jonah 4:2) This is a fact we are reminded of again later in the liturgy, during the season of Lent, when we sing the verse prior to the Gospel reading: "Return to the Lord, your God, for he is gracious and merciful, slow to anger, and abounding in steadfast love."

The Hymn Of Praise

5. *The Gloria In Excelsis is sung (LW)*
7. *The Hymn Of Praise or another appropriate hymn may be sung (LBW)*

When I was a child, I thought it curious that the church seemed so out of step when it came to Christmas music. In my daily world I became accustomed to hearing Christmas carols often starting before Thanksgiving, but in church I heard somber Advent hymns until Christmas. And then came the overdue, and by that time, worn out Christmas carols. Coming belatedly like the colorful wrappers and ribbons discarded and in the trash, the church finally sang Christmas carols. I wondered why the church didn't get with it and do it right. It did not even occur to me that Christmas was more the property of the church than the department stores.

Singing antiquated songs like the *Twelve Days of Christmas* did not make any sense to me. I have no recollection of ever being taught that there truly are 12 days of Christmas (from Christmas to Epiphany [January 6]) in the church year. In our culture, the commercialization of Christmas is deeply entrenched. Every year, as pastor, I struggle to hold off celebrating Christmas until as soon before Christmas as possible. Every year it gets harder to truly celebrate Christmas on Christmas because the day itself is seldom used for worship by modern Lutherans. We have enshrined the god of family, friends and entertainment on the manger of Christmas day.

The first Hymn Of Praise is from the Christmas story. It is the song of the angels when Jesus was born as recorded in Luke 2:14. "Glory to God in the highest, and peace to his people on earth," they sang. And we sing this hymn of praise to God as well — at least usually.

Another "may" rubric. Like the Kyrie, the Hymn Of Praise, can be omitted — especially during penitential seasons of the church year (Advent and Lent). Also, like the Kyrie, the Hymn Of Praise (the "Glory to God" one) is ancient — first mentioned in the fourth century, but assumed to have been in place much earlier than that).

Luther said this Hymn Of Praise "did not grow, nor was it made on earth, but it came down from heaven." Again, as the Kyrie, Apostolic Greeting and the Invocation before, the Hymn Of Praise is addressed to the Trinity. Originally this was a hymn to God the Creator; God the highest. Just as Christmas may be thought of as a gift from God the Creator, so the hymn of the angels sung at Christmas, is a hymn of praise to the Gift-Giver.

The Gift given, however, is none less than Jesus Christ, the Redeemer. And, the way we receive this Gift is through the action of the Holy Spirit, the Sanctifier. So in this hymn we praise "God in the highest . . . Lord God, heavenly king, almighty God . . . " But then we also sing to the "Lord Jesus Christ, only Son of the Father, Lord God, Lamb of God," and to "the Holy Spirit, in the glory of God . . . "

Christmas Island is a little dot of an island in the Indian Ocean, 190 miles south of Java. Its total area is only about 60 square miles and it has never played an important role in history. It got its name and only claim to fame by being discovered on Christmas Day.

To many of us, Christmas itself is only an island — off shore, remote, isolated, and set apart from daily life. The Christmas season is marked by commercial interests (who, if they could, would commercialize Easter more and would love to make something of Pentecost to increase sales). It is an occasion of sometimes artificial joy and good will and peace.

It is a time to cuddle the baby Jesus. It is a child's season. The Hymn Of Praise, "Glory to God" helps us make Christmas a part of our daily lives and helps us define Christmas on its own terms: a gift of our Creator that grants to us eternal life, forgiveness, and true peace. Because of this great gift, we are moved to sing joyfully to this blessed Trinity.

"Glory to God" emphasizes the Christmas theme. The *Lutheran Book Of Worship* also has "This is the Feast" which centers on Easter. On Easter Sunday, after all the flurry of morning worship, our family has always gathered to celebrate with a meal. For many years our immediate family was separated from our extended family and it was impossible to gather and celebrate the bonds that are "family." So the celebration was a distant family gathering. We knew our extended family was together, and our immediate family was also connected by the simultaneous gathering which was further cemented by a long-distance phone call. Sometimes we gathered with friends who took us in and made us, for one Easter afternoon, "family."

"This is the Feast" is the gathering of family — the family of God. "This is the Feast" is the Easter celebration because "the Lamb who was slain" is worthy of receiving our praise. It is a "feast" even though it be simple bread and wine. It is a "feast" because gathering around food is a natural, basic human response to celebrating. When we celebrate a birthday, we have cake and ice cream. When we celebrate a wedding, we have wedding cake and punch. When we celebrate any major rite of passage, we enjoy food. Usually it is simple food too.

This "feast" we celebrate long-distance because it is a celebration with all the saints who have ever lived. It is a mystical commemoration with all those loved ones who have passed on to glory. It is a feast with the great saints of the church. It is a celebration in which the host is none other than Jesus Christ himself who promised to be present wherever only two or three are gathered in his name.

The rite of passage we celebrate is the passage from death to life. The Lamb who was slain has begun his reign. It is a new age in which death no longer has the final word.

The song of joy we sing has the Hebrew word "alleluia" which is a four syllable song of joy in and of itself. The word is found in many psalms — especially in the section from Psalm 113-118, which is called the "Great Alleluia," the latter part of which our Lord likely chanted with his disciples as they gathered at that last supper before his death.

"Alleluia" comes from "Hallelujah" which means "God (JAH) be praised (HALLEL)!" Most modern translations go ahead and translate the phrase into English.

God certainly does not need our praise. God does not need affirmation as we human beings need praise. God simply is. God's nature will not change one iota because of our praise to this wonderful God. But we need to praise God. We need to look again and again at what God has done and sing songs of glory to God in the highest. And thus we make Easter a regular part of our weekly celebration and Christmas a part of ourselves and not some island set aside once a year from Thanksgiving (or earlier) to Christmas Eve.

Chapter
Four

The Prayer Of The Day

6. *The Collect Of The Day is chanted or said; the salutation may precede it. (LW)*
8. *The Prayer Of The Day is said; the salutation may precede it. (LBW)*

P: The Lord be with you.
C: And with your spirit. (LW)
C: And also with you. (LBW)

The Collect or Prayer Of The Day is the bridge between the introductory portions of the worship service and the meat of the service itself.

When Ben was called up for active duty during the Gulf War, his parents took him to the airport. Mom cried and Dad hugged his son and said, "God be with you, Ben." He meant it: "God protect and attend you son. You are important to us and we love you very much. We sincerely wish you God's benevolent protection." That had always been the attitude of

Ben's parents. They have continually loved him. When he went off to school in the mornings as an eight-year-old, they said the same thing only they shortened it. They said "Goodbye." "Goodbye" meant nothing more than a formalized way of departing. But behind that little word which is a shortened version of "God be with you," is an attitude of love and blessing.

The Salutation is like that. More often than not, it is taken for granted. Those words, "The Lord be with you . . . And also with you," come and go and mean little to either party. But one of the purposes of this book is to look again at what we do and ask, "Can't it be more meaningful?" The Salutation is an important blessing.

The Salutation usually comes before the Prayer of the Day (note the "may" rubric). The Salutation (Latin for "health") stems from the Hebrew form of greeting. One first notices that the word "salute" is incorporated. When we think of salute, we usually think of a military greeting. Think of the "salute" in the book of Ruth (2:4) when Boaz came from Bethlehem and said to the reapers, "The Lord be with you" and they answered, "The Lord bless you." Or the "salute" Mary received from the angel. (Luke 1:28) Paul also expressed various "salutes" in his writings. Because of biblical precedent, the "salute" became common from the early days of the church.

The minister says, "The Lord be with you." In other words: "My hope for you people of God is that God our Lord would be in this place among us and that what I do and say would enable you to hear, see, and experience the presence of the divine."

It is an awesome and humbling thing for the minister to hear the entire congregation respond, "AND WITH YOUR SPIRIT" (*LW*) or "AND ALSO WITH YOU" (*LBW*). Here the minister "confidently abandons self to the Lord," as one writer put it, humbly displacing self and depending upon the presence of God for the awesome duties of Christian worship.

The Salutation is further preparation for true worship of God. It almost seems like an interruption in the flow of the service. The Invocation, Confession, Greeting, Hymn of the

Day, Kyrie, and Hymn of Praise is suddenly broken by another greeting of sorts. Actually, it is more like a crescendo in the service. The Salutation is saying, "Listen. The prayer and readings that follow are important. We have been preparing ourselves to hear our Lord, now we do so."

In ancient times among some of the Greeks there was even more of a break in the flow as a deacon would stand in the front and shout, "The doors, the doors." He would direct the catechumens, the penitents, and those under discipline to leave at this point. Only those in full standing in the church are privileged to hear what is about to follow.

From ancient times there has been a silence at this point. The silence says, "It is time to collect our thoughts. The preparation is over. Let us hear the word of the Lord."

Then comes the Prayer Of The Day. *Lutheran Worship* calls this the Collect because that is exactly the function of this prayer: to collect the thoughts of the assembly into one central theme — the Prayer of the day. This is the final portion of the entrance rite.

These prayers articulating the theme of the day are found in the front part of the worship book (pages 10-123 in *Lutheran Worship*; pages 13-41 in the *Lutheran Book Of Worship*). *Lutheran Worship* calls these the PROPERS OF THE DAY. Listed with the prayer is the Introit, the appointed scripture Readings, the Gradual, and the Verse. A "proper" is a variable part of the weekly liturgy. These parts change each week within the structure of the weekly service.

For 15 centuries the church has collected the thought and spirit of the weekly worship service in the Collect. These terse, brilliant prayers connect the worshiper with the saints of the ages as well as with contemporary saints. Throughout time these prayers have been refined and perfected by the church. Reed notes "The perfect collect is an art form the poetic values of which are expressed not in rhymed words but in rhymed thoughts, arranged in definite patterns of rhythmic prose. The essential merit of the collect is its spiritual content, its forthrightness, fervor, and sincerity."[5] He quotes Loehe, a leader in appreciating the Collects in the middle of the 19th century, who spoke of them as "the breath of a soul, sprinkled with the blood of Jesus, brought to the eternal Father in the Name of his Son."

The earliest name for the Collect was simply *Oratio* — "the prayer." The name Collect probably dates from the early Roman custom of gathering for worship with a prayer. The weekly prayer is usually related in thought to the Gospel reading of the day. Its chief function today is the same as it has been since the earliest days of Christianity: to prepare those who worship for the readings that follow. Some of these prayers are ancient in origin and reflect the remarkable stability of worship through controversy, revolution, and reformation.

Most of the Prayers Of The Day or Collects follow a special structure of five parts: 1. an **Address**, 2. a **Basis for prayer**, 3. the **Petition**, 4. the **Benefit desired**, and 5. the **Conclusion**. The Prayer Of The Day for Easter shows this structure:

Address	O God,
Basis for prayer	you gave your only Son to suffer death on the cross for our redemption, and by his glorious resurrection you delivered us from the power of death.
Petition	Make us die every day to sin,
Benefit desired	so that we may live with him forever in the joy of the resurrection;
Conclusion	through Jesus Christ our Lord, who lives and reigns with you and the Holy Spirit, one God, now and forever. Amen.

Sometimes the second or fourth part is missing. Occasionally both may be absent from the prayer. Most of the prayers begin by addressing the First Person of the Trinity. Many address the Lord. None in our Lutheran books of worship address the Holy Spirit. All end similarly "through Jesus Christ our Lord ... " Most frequently the appeal at the end is to the Trinitarian God we worship. The Collects in the *Lutheran Book Of Worship* tend to be more concise than those in *Lutheran Worship*. The prayers in both are essentially the same, ancient supplications, but they are based on different translations.

The Prayer Of The Day or Collect is introduced the same way — the minister says, "Let us pray ... " The Latin word for this is *Oremus*. The congregation joins in saying or singing **"Amen"** at the conclusion of the prayer. The Prayer itself is a "presidential prayer"[6] given only to the presiding minister. The congregation does not normally pray this prayer in unison.

The Lessons

Sit

7. *The Old Testament Reading ... is announced. (LW)*
9. *The First Lesson is announced and read. (LBW)*

9. *The Gradual For The Season or the appointed Psalm is sung or said. (LW)*
11. *The appointed Psalm is sung or said. (LBW)*

10. *The Epistle is announced. (LW)*
12. *The Second Lesson is announced and read. (LBW)*

Years ago, the Lutheran service limited itself mostly to the New Testament. Now the rubrics say "The First Lesson **IS** announced and read." The "First Lesson" is almost always from the Old Testament! *Lutheran Worship* says it plainly.

Not many years ago the Lutheran service limited itself in the number of Psalms read or sung. Now the Psalm is sung or read in most of our churches most of the time! Luther called the Psalter "a little Bible" because "In it is comprehended most beautifully and briefly everything that is in the entire

73

Bible."[7] The Psalms have been used by God's people for millennia. Usually they were sung. Most Lutheran parishes now sing the psalms as well.

It is right that our services get back to the Lessons. This was a feature of early Christian worship as it was worship in the synagogue of Jesus' day. There is that poignant story of Jesus beginning his ministry in his home town of Nazareth: "He stood up to read, and the scroll of the prophet Isaiah was given to him. He unrolled the scroll and found that place where it was written ... And he rolled up the scroll ... and sat down." He began with the Lessons. (Luke 4:16-21)

When Jesus died, rose and ascended, he left the church in the power of Pentecost with the fulfilled promise of a "Comforter" — the Holy Spirit. With the church's birth, certain Jewish customs continued such as the tradition of reading the Lessons at worship. Gradually the church added letters sent by the apostles (the word Apostle means "One who is sent"). These letters were preserved, copied, read and reread in churches across the then-known world. Most of them came from the Apostle Paul. Many Christians don't realize that the letters (we used to call them "epistles") were the earliest portions of what we now call the New Testament. They were directly from the Apostles. In fact, in the early church, the "epistle" reading was called the "apostle" reading. The epistle readings always come before the gospel readings as the lesser precedes the greater. Medieval thought considered the epistle readings as being like the ministry of John the Baptist, who "went before" the Lord to "prepare the way." The Gospels: Matthew, Mark, Luke and John came later as the oral stories about Jesus — his teachings, miracles, opposition from the authorities, death and resurrection — were set to written words.

There are four sets of lessons: The Old Testament readings (the First Lesson), followed by the Psalm (which is actually an ancient, Old Testament hymn), then the epistle reading (the Second Lesson). After the second lesson **"The appointed VERSE is sung by the choir, or the congregation may sing the appropriate Verse ..."** and the Gospel is announced and read.

One writer suggested that the First and Second Lesson are instructions from God our Creator; the Gospel is the voice of God the Redeemer (Jesus); and the Sermon is from the Holy Spirit (via the lips of the preacher). Here again we return to the Trinity in the liturgy of the Lutheran Church.

The entire first part of the Lutheran service is a service of the Word. The "Word" uses words. That is a problem with many people today because we live in a post-literate society.

It had been suggested that we live in a time when many people can relate more to images, movement, and pictures rather than words. Such was the case in Jesus' day (and before him, Moses' day). It is not accidental that Jesus used sensory images to preach, speak and teach. He talked about the birds of the air, the grains of wheat and the chaff, the whitewashed tombs, and images of banquets, lost coins, and found sons. The people Jesus spoke to could relate to images better than to words. This is one reason there was no apparent hurry in getting the gospels in written form. The oral storyteller was trusted and known to be accurate (true to this day in societies rich in oral tradition).

Over time the world changed and more and more people learned to read. With the invitation of moveable type by Johann Gutenberg in 1440, printing became an inexpensive way to duplicate words so that increasingly more people could relate to written words. The first book printed was a Bible. It is interesting that Gutenberg's invention was perhaps Martin Luther's greatest aid in calling attention to his concerns. Luther's *Ninety-Five Theses* were copied and printed; distributed and read throughout the then-known world. This fact probably saved Luther's life and certainly gave Luther a vastly wider audience than predecessor reformers.

The Lutheran church was born in the midst of this revolution of the mass media. Suddenly lay people had Bibles in their own languages and eventually even in their own homes. We take this so much for granted today that we can scarcely appreciate what a radical and wonderful thing this was and how it turned the world around. Choirs shared their music with the congregation; preachers shared the liturgy with the people in the pew.

For more than 400 years we have been a largely literate society where more people learned to read and become familiar with words. Lutheran hymnals and liturgies were printed, read and learned by millions of people. One has to be literate to be Lutheran. At one time that was a compliment and favorable statement about Lutherans. Now, however, it says that we are exclusive. Many people cannot read and to pretend otherwise is to ignore reality. Furthermore we have an aging population that often cannot see as well.

Of even more significance than illiteracy and eyesight problems is the revolution that has occurred in these modern times — ever since the television set reacquainted us to images over words and the dominance of the senses over thought and imagination. I say this not as a judgment, but as an observation and statement of the way the world has changed and left us with a liturgy that is often foreign to the way the majority of people in the world today experience truth and reality.

One of the purposes of this book is to give the reader the images and pictures lacking in the mere words of our liturgy. The liturgy is still valid, but must be approached from a different perspective. The preacher's challenge is to enliven the written word in visual, auditory, and other sensory images that relates to where people are today. That is a mighty challenge and requires that the minister understand the written word as well as the lives of the people in the pews while submitting to the guidance of the Holy Spirit.

When I was a young man I often wondered why I always heard about "Bible study." "Why not just read the Bible," I thought. "Why must it be a 'study?' " Literary works have "readings" but so often the Bible comes through a "study." Later reflection helped me understand why it must be a study. Bible reading, as one would read a newspaper, cannot be done. It just does not make sense. Or, if it does make sense, it is probably a misinterpretation of the text! Understanding the Bible is hard work. That is probably why so many Bibles are sitting around peoples' homes going unread. It is easier and more comfortable to assume one knows what is in the Bible than it is to dig in and find out what the Bible is really saying.

Commentaries, maps, dictionaries, an understanding of the language, the culture in which the Bible was written are all helpful in comprehending the text. The Bible, despite the best of modern translations, is demanding upon any reader. It requires study, not just surface reading.

The Lessons are read in worship and I suspect they get switched off in most hearers' minds. That is why so many Lutheran churches not only read the lessons, but encourage worshipers to follow along with the lessons printed on the back of the bulletin or in an insert.

The Lessons come from a book called a "Lectionary." Lectionaries contain portions of the Bible that are read on appointed Sundays. They have been around since the beginning of the church when it met the synagogues of Judaism which had readings from the Law and the Prophets. The early Christian church continued with these Jewish readings and added the letters of the apostles — probably first informally and then formally. Later came readings from the Gospels. This threefold reading of Old Testament, letters, and Gospels coordinated nicely with the Trinity again. Over time, however, the Old Testament lesson was dropped in many of the Christian churches.

At first the readings were read, as one of the early church leaders (Justin Martyr) wrote, "as long as time permits." Most lectors today would not get by with reading that long. I went to a convocation recently where the speaker read his speech — a brilliant exposition. This lasted for just half an hour and the people were outraged! Ministers who read their sermons receive similar reproach. The clock has a prominent place in today's church. Many people in the pews are anxious about time and schedules. Futhermore, as we have noted, the read word tends to go right through people's heads.

Over the years of liturgical development certain lessons became associated with specific times of the church year. Pentecost, one of the oldest church celebrations was associated with the reading from the book of Acts which tells what happened on Pentecost when the church was born. Readings about the prophecy of Jesus fit naturally in the Advent season as with the Christmas story at Christmas. The stories of Jesus' last week on this earth coincided consistently during Holy Week. And, of course, the dramatic story of his resurrection was the Easter reading.

Preachers liked using a lectionary because it gave them a coordinated series of lessons that fit with the Prayer of the Day (the "Collect") and gave unity to the service. The lectionary also gave preachers a well-used and thought-out approach that covers the basics in the Bible. Every preacher has a pet subject and were it not for the discipline of the lectionary, would find one's ministry being rather lopsided.

The book with the lessons is called the Lectionary, but the lessons themselves are called the "pericope" (pronounced per-i-cope-e) which comes from a Greek word meaning a portion "cut out." Obviously the lessons are "cut out" of the whole Bible as a representative portion of what the Bible says in its entirety.

Often, in our Lutheran churches, laity read the lessons and the pastor reads the gospel. The lessons give yet another opportunity for the liturgy to be the "work of the people."

In the early days of the church, the congregation met in synagogues and then homes. Several hundred years later the practice of building church buildings began. The buildings faced east toward the rising sun as representative of the hope of Easter and the rising Son, our Lord, Jesus Christ. At the east end of the church, a raised platform dominated by a large, almost square table or altar, caught the attention of the worshiper. The choir was nearby. The clergy sat behind the altar, against the circular wall of the "apse." The celebrant at Holy Communion could stand behind the altar, facing the people. The majority of our Lutheran churches have revived this practice of a free-standing altar.

Between the altar area (called "sanctuary") and the place where the people sat ("nave") were two readings desks ("ambos"). They stood at opposite sides of the church. As one faced the altar, the desk on the right was lower and less ornate. The other, however, was of greater importance in the church's worship.

When the lessons were read, they were read from the south side (on the right of the altar). After reading the lessons, the choir sang a psalm. Then the book containing the Gospels was taken to the ornate desk on the north. As time passed, the desks disappeared and became the lectern and the pulpit. Often the lessons were read from the altar — on the "epistle" (south) side of the sanctuary. The Gospel, however, was read from the "gospel" (north) side. This is still the custom today. The Gospels are given prominence over the lessons. They, after all, contain the sacred story of the One who was the Word. As J. B. Phillips worded it in his paraphrase of the opening chapter of John, "At the beginning God expressed himself." The lessons point to God's expression of the Word, Jesus Christ.

The Gospel

14. The appointed VERSE is sung by the choir, or the congregation may sing the appropriate Verse below.

Stand
  C: Alleluia. Lord, to whom shall we go? You have the words of eternal life. Alleluia.

OR
LENT

C: Return to the Lord, your God, for he is gracious and merciful, slow to anger, and abounding in steadfast love.

Before we ever get to the reading from the gospels, the appointed Verse "is sung" by the choir or the congregation. The old Lutheran liturgies called this verse the "Gradual" which is a Latin word meaning a step *(gradis)*. *Lutheran Worship* has maintained the GRADUAL and placed it after the Old Testament reading as an option to the Psalm. The VERSE in both *Lutheran Worship* and the *Lutheran Book Of Worship* is still a "Gradual" — a step up from the other readings. The whole first part of the liturgy, the "Liturgy of the Word," points to what follows the Verse — the Gospel reading. The Gospel reading is the highlight of the liturgy of the Word. Luther Reed, in his monumental work on the Lutheran liturgy, calls the Gospel "the liturgical summit of the first half of the Service."[8]

The Verse is the transition from the other lessons to the Gospel. The words are those of Peter when the Lord asked if he and the other disciples would desert him as all the others had. "Lord," Peter asks, "To whom shall we go? You have the words of eternal life." (John 6:68) The Gospel reading contains the "words of eternal life."

Peter's question comes to all sincere followers of the Lord. Doubt is as much a part of faith as belief. Henry Drummond once said, "Christ never failed to distinguish between doubt and unbelief. Doubt is *can't believe*; unbelief is *won't believe*. Doubt is honesty; unbelief is obstinacy. Doubt is looking for light; unbelief is content with darkness."

The disciples had their doubts but wondered who or what else to believe. "You, Lord, have the words of eternal life" they concluded. We human beings need to believe in something beyond ourselves. Victor Frankl found that truth in the concentration camps of Nazi Germany. The survivors of those camps were people who had a meaning, a purpose above and beyond themselves. That kept them going, even against incredible odds. In his classic book, *Man's Search for Meaning*, Frankl observed that everyone needs to believe in something beyond himself. Even Nietzsche, the philosopher who declared that God is dead, is quoted as saying that "he who has a *why* to live for can bear with almost any *how*."

So who can give us the great why? As I write this the country is in an election year. Candidates are making promises that no human being occupying the various offices can deliver. Is that where we turn for eternal life? What about modern medical science? Is that where we turn? Perhaps, especially if we want to extend our life. But no matter how much medical science can extend life, even the healthiest of the healthy will someday die. "Words of eternal life?" — not here. So where? If politics and science cannot deliver — then who or what? How about education? If we only get enough educated people, then life shall be perfect. None less than Daniel Webster said:

> *If we work upon marble, it will perish. If we work upon brass, time will efface it. If we rear temples, they will crumble to dust. But if we work upon men's immortal minds, if we imbue them with high principles, with the just fear of God and love of their fellow men, we engrave on those tablets something which no time can efface, and which will brighten and brighten to all eternity.*

So will education do it? Again we have the individual problem of learning great wisdom and achieving tremendous knowledge, only to develop senility and lose recognition even of one's own spouse of 60 years. "Lord, to whom shall we turn?" With Peter, we turn to the Lord. The Verse reverences the One who has those words — Jesus Christ. We rise with the singing of the Verse because in the Gospel we hear the words of eternal life from the One who earned eternal life by his death and resurrection.

This ancient "Gradual" which gradually moves us up a step for a direct encounter with the Lord; has historically been sung by the choir. In the *Minister's Desk Edition* of the *Lutheran Book Of Worship* (which, by the way, is the same as the big, green Altar Edition), a Verse appropriate for each Sunday of the church year is noted. *Lutheran Worship* includes the Gradual and Verse in the Propers. Choirs are encouraged to sing these verses from time to time. In most Lutheran congregations, however, the people sing the words of the hymnal except during Lent. In Lent we encounter the same words of the first lesson of Ash Wednesday. They are from the prophet Joel: "Return to the Lord, your God, for he is gracious and merciful, slow to anger, and abounding in steadfast love." (*LBW*)

Returning to God is the whole focus of Lent. Returning is another word for "repentance." Repentance is an exercise in seeing ourselves for what we are. As Frederick Buechner says, "To repent is to come to your senses. It is not so much something you do as something that happens. True repentance spends less time looking at the past and saying, 'I'm sorry,' than to the future and saying, 'Wow!' "[9] Martin Luther said it this way: "God created the world out of nothing. As long as I am not yet nothing, God cannot make something out of me." Returning to God; repenting, means growing in faith. It means growing in love. It means becoming alive.

So whether we return to the Lord our God or simply turn to the one who has the words of eternal life, we turn with hope of hearing the good news. Both worship books include the Hebrew word Alleluia in the Verse. Certainly such praise to God is appropriate. Alleluia, as you recall, means, "Praise the Lord." Praising God is as natural as breathing to the person about to hear again the wonderful news of Jesus Christ.

The word Gospel is derived from the Greek meaning "good news." Good news it is! The reading of the Gospel is the representation of the presence of Christ himself among us. The reading is done by the presiding pastor. At its reading everyone able rises. In the ancient church at this point soldiers laid down their swords and the bishop removed his mitre. Even the emperor or king removed his crown. The reading of the Gospel is reminiscent of how the King first rose upon hearing Handel's "Hallelujah Chorus." Now all rise at this stirring chorus of Handel's because it points beyond the composer. It suggests a reality far beyond the chorus and the orchestra. It lifts up a truth beyond time and place. It points to the good news of Jesus Christ. Such is the Gospel reading today.

When the President of the United States enters a room, the people rise out of respect. When people are introduced to one another, they usually rise — again out of respect. So much more we rise to honor the Lord of the Church; the Lord of the service, Jesus Christ.

The Gospel reading is from one of the four "gospels" as we call them: Matthew, Mark, Luke or John. The modern lectionary divides the readings among the three synoptic gospels and the Gospel of John. We call Matthew, Mark, and Luke "synoptic" because they "see-with" each other. What is in one is likely in another. The Greek word *syn* equals "with" and *optic* equals "see." John's Gospel is in a class by itself. Written much later than the synoptics, it has material usually not included in the other three. Often John is called "the Fourth Gospel."

The lectionary gives us a full opportunity to experience the Gospel from every angle. Year A has a predominance of readings from Matthew; B from Mark; and C from Luke. Since Mark is shorter than the other synoptics and contains less teaching material, Series B is replete with passages from the Gospel of John. Readings from John are found in all three years — especially during the Easter season.

When the minister reads the Gospel, listen. Hear the words. Imagine Jesus himself has entered the sanctuary and is now standing before you and speaking to YOU. Lay aside every distraction. Focus. Hear. Observe. Let the Gospel become good news to you.

The Sermon

Its been said that a sermon can help people in different ways. Some rise from it greatly strengthened, others wake from it deeply refreshed. Some years back, a reader of *The British Weekly* wrote this provocative letter to the editor:

> *Dear Sir:*
> *It seems ministers feel their sermons are very important and spend a great deal of time preparing them. I have been attending a church service quite regularly for the*

*past 30 years and I have probably heard 3,000 of them.
To my consternation, I discovered that I cannot remember a single sermon. I wonder if a minister's time might
be more profitably spent on something else?*

Perhaps quite a few people have wondered the same thing.
Preaching is often not remembered, even by the preacher.
Sometimes we wonder if it does any good.

In the early days of the church, the sermon was tremendously important. But over time its prominence lessened in
Christian worship. It had really lost favor in the church until
the Reformation restored it to its proper place. Over the years
the sermon has increased and decreased in importance like a
yo-yo. During some times in the history of the church, the sermon lasted hours. In modern times, with competition from
professionals on television and radio and with media-
conditioned attention spans, most sermons are less than half
an hour. I know of one minister who says categorically, ''If
the sermon is longer than ten minutes, I can guarantee you
that most of the congregation is not listening.''

The sermon is not a lecture or speech. It is a unique form
of literature. Reed says, ''the Sermon is the voice of the living
church lifted in instruction, testimony and exhortation.''[10] It
is part of the liturgy. It fits in with the rest of the service
although Luther at first thought the sermon should be at the
beginning of the service so that it not interrupt the flow of
the liturgy. Time has shown that the sermon fits nicely where
it is situated in the liturgy.

In the sermon the minister expounds on the lessons. Most
Lutheran ministers have received years of training in Greek
and Hebrew — the languages of scripture, biblical history, and
other knowledge to enable faithful application of the text to
the modern situation. Every preacher preparing for the sermon is bound to consult commentaries, biblical dictionaries,
atlases, and other aids so that the proclaimer of the word faithfully conveys God's word and not mere opinion. This is not
a time for the preacher to use the pulpit for a favorite topic.

This is the time to relate the texts to modern life. How does the ancient word of the Lord in Scripture apply to the daily grind of modern times? That is the preacher's challenge.

Since the sermon is but a part of the Lutheran liturgy, the temptation among clergy is to let the sermon slide off to the side of the weekly schedule of things to do. "After all," the preacher says, "the Word is present in the liturgy and 'God's word shall not return void.' " (Isaiah 55:11) But in congregation after congregation, especially as they consider who to call as their pastor, good preaching is almost always the number one quality people look for in their pastor. As one call committee member said, "If the pastor has it together in preaching, chances are he also has it together in other areas of ministry as well."

The sermon is the living word proclaimed in modern terms. As such it is heralded from the pulpit. In Lutheran churches the pulpit is situated to the side of the chancel area. In the many Lutheran churches I have been in over the years, I have never yet seen the pulpit anywhere but off to the side — whereas this is not the case in many other protestant churches. There is a reason for that. The sermon, while important and representative of the living word of Christ, is still human-oriented. The focus in the Lutheran Church is always God-ward. It is God's action in baptism that counts most — not our meager offerings; not our "decision" for Christ. The central visual focus of the sanctuary is the altar and the cross on or above it. It is what God has done in Christ that matters, not our human actions.

The pastor often begins the sermon the way one of the apostles greeted his congregation — with the apostolic greeting: "Grace, mercy and peace be to you from God the Father and our Lord and Savior Jesus Christ." Sometimes the pastor may begin "In the name of the Father, and of the Son and of the Holy Spirit. Amen." Others simply begin.

By the way, the letter to *The British Weekly* about the writer not remembering any of the 3,000 sermons he had heard, received this rebuttal letter published a couple of weeks later:

Dear Sir:
I have been married for 30 years. During that time I have eaten 32,850 meals — mostly of my wife's cooking. Suddenly, I have discovered that I cannot remember the menu of a single meal. And yet, I received nourishment from every single one of them. I have the distinct impression that without them, I would have starved to death long ago.

Perhaps it is such with preaching as well!

Chapter
Five

The Hymn

Some people don't like music. President U. S. Grant said "I only know two tunes. One is 'Yankee Doodle' and the other isn't." George Bernard Shaw liked music, but he was particular. He didn't care for music while eating. Once, while attending a dinner party where a band played, he asked the conductor, "Could you play something if I asked you to?"

"Of course," beamed the smiling musician.

"Well, would you either play poker or dominoes at least until I'm through eating?"

On another occasion, Shaw attended a concert by a violinist. "Well, what did you think of the violinist?" a man asked.

"He reminded me of Paderewski," Shaw replied.

"But," hesitated the man, "Paderewski is not a violinist."

"And neither is this man," the playwright answered.

Most of us like music. Even those of us not so talented musically, whistle, hum, or sing in the shower. When we gather at birthday celebrations, we don't think twice about singing

"Happy Birthday" to the honored guest. Sometimes at ball games we dare sing the "Star Spangled Banner." Other than that, when do we sing with others? Congregational singing in church is a wonderful opportunity!

Prior to Luther's Reformation, there was little congregational singing in the church. It was discouraged and barely tolerated. The other reformers of Luther's day were inclined to disparage congregational singing. They saw it as a potentially troublesome experiment that needed close supervision. Not Luther! After the Gospel itself, Luther saw music as God's great gift to humankind. He called music a "noble, wholesome, and joyful creation." It is a true gift of God. Surely, as one hears the wonderful word of the Gospel, the heart's inclination is toward music. "If any would not sing and talk of what Christ has wrought for us, he shows thereby that he does not really believe," Luther wrote.

Notice the direction, the inclination in Luther's view of music. It fits the rest of the Lutheran service. Music is not something WE devise — it is God's gift! The orientation is outward from the Source: God. As surely as the words of scripture, liturgy, and sermon inspire and direct as instruments of God, so does music and art. God uses these gifts. It is no accident that some of the great masterpieces of music and art originated within the church. One immediately thinks of Michelangelo's Sistine Chapel frescoes or the architectural wonders of cathedrals such as the Cologne Cathedral or Notre Dame in Paris. Sculptors like Bernini; painters like Titian all created their masterpieces for the church. Then there are the great musicians like Bach and poets like Newton who formulate their artistry for the glory of God. God speaks to us of "good news" through the arts as surely as through the written and proclaimed word.

Lutheran organist Paul Manz said it well: "The church musician is one who is always called to *minister* to people, but in a unique way. To be sure, he does preach and he does teach. Yes, he also comforts the bereaved, and he helps to sustain the weak. Often he counsels the troubled and distressed, and he always assists at the distribution of the Sacraments. He does all this, but *never* from the altar, lectern, pulpit, or font, but from the choir loft and organ bench. Futhermore, he does this all in a nonverbal manner in spite of the fact that we have been led to believe that *all* theological and liturgical communication is verbal. Certainly it is not, as both music and art so ably demonstrate."[11]

The Hymn of the Day is the chief hymn of the service. It is either immediately before or after the sermon because it, too, is a comment on the readings and the sermon in relation to the church year. The Hymn of the Day often fits with the sermon and may be a preparation for it. With some congregations, the hymn supports the sermon and immediately follows. This is perhaps preferable since the sermon, which is an exposition on the texts, has more impact when following the reading. That impact is lessened when a hymn comes between.

Lutherans use the hymns, especially the Hymn of the Day, for liturgical purposes and not just so the congregation has something to do. The words and the music all fit the theme of the day.

The Creed

15. *The CREED. The Nicene Creed is said at celebrations of Holy Communion and on major festivals; the Apostles' Creed at other times. The Creeds may be sung (see Canticles and Chants, No. 4, and Hymns 212 and 213). (LW)*

20. *The CREED may be said. The Nicene Creed is said on all festivals and on Sundays in the seasons of Advent, Christmas, Lent, and Easter. The Apostles' Creed is said at other times. The Creed is omitted here if the service of Holy Baptism or another rite with a creed is used. (LBW)*

These days corporations and organizations develop "Mission Statements" to define what they are and do. Churches often do the same and even individuals and families have found "Mission Statements" helpful in identifying exactly who one is and what one does. The Creed is the universal church's Mission Statement. The Creed has been in existence for hundreds and hundreds of years — long before the idea of Mission Statements came into vogue.

The word Creed comes from the Latin *Credo* which means "I believe." We have three Creeds in the Lutheran Church: The Apostles', Nicene, and Athanasian. All three stress the one God, three persons concept of the Trinity. Most of us are familiar with the Apostles' and Nicene Creeds — they say roughly the same thing. But the Athanasian Creed is something else again. Older Lutheran worship books did not even bother to include it as our *Lutheran Worship* and *Lutheran Book Of Worship* have.

It is seldom, if ever, used liturgically. Even a casual reading quickly reveals why this Creed is not used every Sunday (and in many of our churches not used at all). It is long and repetitious — saying over and over again in as many ways as possible that God is one entity in three persons. The focus of the Athanasian Creed is the Trinity more than anything. This Creed, if said at all, is said on Trinity Sunday when that concept is uppermost in the minds of worshipers.

Why? Why have a creed? Many rapidly growing churches today say, "Let the Spirit decide what one believes ... We don't need a written creed." Some proudly boast, "The Bible is our creed." Others say the Creed is just words piled on words. Don't we have enough of words? Enough already!

Churches without a Creed often are very individualistic and subjective. It was precisely this individualism and subjectivity that led the church to develop Creeds in the first place. Today we have groups like the Mormons who want to appear to be Christian. They are not. They cannot recite the measure of Christianity: the Creed. "Christian" Science and other groups and sects with the word "Christian" in them are not, in fact, Christian. We know that because we have a measure, a norm — the Creed. The early church needed such a measure as well.

There were people who claimed to have a special, secret revelation from God and they, therefore, were MORE Christian than others. Others denied some very basic elements of Christianity such as the humanity of Christ or the divinity of our Lord. The church had to make a decision about what is orthodox and what is not. The Creed is the result and the answer.

In A.D. 325 a council of representatives from all over the church met in the city of Nicea. There the controversy in which the church found itself and which threatened to tear it apart was discussed and the question uppermost on everyone's mind was: "What does it mean to be Christian?" The Scripture was the measuring stick, the guide. It was distilled and put into a belief statement that has taken its name after the city in which it was formulated: Nicea. This creed, revised at Constantinople some years later, is essentially the one we have in our Lutheran worship books.

Furthermore the church realized a long time ago that it really does matter what one believes. Recently the newspapers carried a report about five religious cultists convicted in the exorcism death of a three-year-old boy whom they were accused of beating to death to rid him of the devil.

A 51-year-old man who was a self-professed minister to the religious household, the dead boy's 20-year-old mother, and the minister's stepdaughter were among those convicted. The boy was found in September, an estimated two months after he had died. His body was in a sealed-off bedroom in the cult's home in Washington state.

The defendants maintained they spanked rather than beat the boy, because they believed he was possessed by the devil. The minister said they expected the boy to be resurrected. This is why they kept him in the home. The child's mother testified that he died after she had dropped him to the floor and he "growled" at her. She said she was convinced he was possessed by the devil and that it was the devil, not her son, who gave up the body. She was simply waiting his return from the dead when arrested.

These were God-believing people — sincere in every way. But wrong! Stories like this and others like Jonestown and the Temple Davidian cults which ended in tragedy remind us that our beliefs matter. The Church decided long ago that it is important for us to understand God as One God in three personalities; three modes of approach to us human beings.

The third and perhaps the most-used is the Apostles' Creed. The Apostles' Creed was not written by the apostles as we might conclude from its title, but it comes from the earliest days of Christianity even though it didn't take its present form until 750 A.D. It is an expansion of Matthew 28:19: "Go therefore and make disciples of all nations, baptizing them in the name of the Father and of the Son and of the Holy Spirit." An early church legend, recorded by Rufinus of Aquileia around the year 400 A.D. states that at Pentecost, the Holy Spirit gave the Apostles the ability to speak and understand every language on earth. As the Apostles gathered together before departing to the four corners of the earth, they decided to settle on a common form of expressing the basics of the faith they professed. The Apostles' Creed, the legend says, is the result.

The legend may or may not be true. The oldest written Creed we have comes from shortly after the year 100 A.D. This Creed is very close to the Apostles' and was used as a baptismal creed in which candidates for baptism professed their belief. Our current Apostles' Creed (as well as the Nicene and Athanasian) surely had its origins from the days of the apostles themselves even though we have no proof that the apostles wrote it in its current form.

In the early days as in these latter, the Creed was a basic educational tool on the essentials of the Christian faith. It says in summary form what we believe. It is not in the Bible except that it is derived from the teachings in the Bible. It is a distillation of the basics. To this day the Creed is a wonderful teaching and preaching tool.

Lutheran Worship maintains the singular pronoun "I" in the Apostles' and Nicene Creeds. The *Lutheran Book Of Worship* uses the pronouns to make a significant point. The

Apostles' Creed uses first person "I believe . . ." Since it is the Creed of Holy Baptism, this should be expected. No one can believe for another. No one can be baptized on behalf of another. No one can profess his or her faith for another. Each of us must answer for him or herself. In the Nicene Creed the *Lutheran Book Of Worship* departs from *Lutheran Worship* to emphasize the communal function of the Creed by using the plural "we" in stating the Christian belief.

The Creed, whether using the singular "I" or the plural "we" does the same thing: it binds one person to another in community. The community is called the church. William Barclay, in his book *The Apostles' Creed For Everyman*, points out that an individual may not understand everything about the Creed and may even doubt things the Creed professes, and still say it with utter integrity because the person unites with God's people in the affirmation of this statement of the faith, "even if there are parts of it about which he has doubts or reservations or even denials."[12]

The *Lutheran Book Of Worship* Creed talks about "the holy catholic Church." *Lutheran Worship* uses "catholic" as an alternative. Instead it uses "Christian" to emphasize the universal church. The use of the word "catholic" is often misunderstood even though it has ancient roots. If "catholic" is not a capital letter, it means "universal." A capitalized "Catholic" refers to one of the Catholic denominations — usually *Roman* Catholic. In the Creed we bind ourselves to that community which extends beyond this place and even this time — the holy, catholic church. It is a community "of saints" that includes those believers who have come before and those that follow! That's quite a church! It's a church much larger than our Lutheran Church. It is a secret church known only to God to be revealed at the final judgment because only God can see into the hearts, minds and souls of individuals. God knows who the real church members are — and they aren't necessarily just those with names on our Lutheran church rolls!

The minister leads the recital of the Creed from his or her seat. The Creed is a response to the whole proclamation of the Word of God. The Nicene Creed is most closely associated with the celebration of Holy Communion and also with more solemn or festive services. The Apostles' Creed is more frequently used when the color of the day is green.

The rubrics say the Creed "may" be said. If there is a baptism, for example, it would be repetitious to say the Creed here in the service as well as later, during the baptism. Also the Creed could be omitted for those days that are less festive. Omitting it from time to time actually empahsizes it and keeps it from being a merely repetitious act. The Creed may also be sung to Luther's hymn entitled "We All Believe in One True God" to give variety to the service.

Prayer

Never seen weather so powerful dry —
*   Burnt up the hill an' the plain;*
An' I say to the deacon: "We'll perish," says I;
*   "We'd better be prayin' for rain."*
An' "You're right," says the deacon, An' so we got down
An' soon had 'em prayin' all over the town!

They prayed before breakfas', petitioned at noon:
*   "Good Lord, sen' the rain, sen' the rain!*
We hain't had a drop since the middle o' June —
*   The dry drought has ruint the grain.*
The hills are on fire, an' the heat up on high
Is makin' big cracks in the blue o' the sky!"

They prayed in the mornin' and hollered all night,
*   'Till at last come the ghost of a cloud —*
A rollin' o' thunder — a flashin' o' light,
*   An' the big rain all over the crowd!*
It swelled up the rivers, it deluged the town —
An' still the mean Angels kep' flingin' it down!

Never seen weather so powerful wet!
  Ruint the corn an' the rye;
An' I says to the deacon: "We're sufferin' yet,
  We'd better be prayin' for dry!"
An' "You're right," says the deacon, An' so we got down
An' soon had 'em prayin' all over the town!
    — "Prayin' For Rain" by Frank L. Stanton

What is this thing we call "Prayer?" Some might say it's just a mere wishing and talking to the air. Some might say praying is nothing and gets you nowhere. "Praying," they say, "is magical, childish, wishing — nothing more."

Praying is merely talking with God. That's it! Nothing complicated here. Any child can do it. One can do it any way one wants. Let me share another ridiculous poem about prayer:

"The proper way for man to pray," said Deacon Lemeul
  Keyes:
"The only proper attitude is down upon his knees."
"Nay I should say the way to pray," said Reverend
  Doctor Wide,
"Is standing straight with out stretched arms with rapt
  and upturned eyes."
"Oh, no, no, no," said Elder Snow "Such posture is too
  proud.

"A man should pray with eyes fast closed and head
  contritely bowed."
"It seems to me hands should be austerely clasped in front
With both thumbs pointing to the ground," said
  Reverend Doctor Blunt.

"Last year I fell in Hodgkin's well headfirst," said Cyril
  Brown
"With both my heels a-stickin' up, my head a pointin'
  down;
And I done prayed right then and there, best prayer I
  ever said.
The prayin'est prayer I ever prayed, a-standin' on my
  head."

Whether praying on our knees, on our feet, head bowed, arms stretched out or up-side-down, prayer is merely talking with God. Not talking to God; talking with God.

Harry Emerson Fosdick wrote that "We hammer so busily that the architect cannot discuss the plans with us. We are so preoccupied with the activities of sailing, that we do not take our bearings from the sky ... Even a casual study of the effective servants of the world reveals how much of their vision and stimulus came in quiet and receptive hours. Prayer gave God his opportunity to speak, for prayer is the listening ear."

Two Air Force pilots shot out of the skies of Vietnam were sharing their memories. One asked the other, "What were you thinking about when you were shot down over Vietnam and were parachuting to earth?" The other replied, "I prayed as I had never prayed before." The first pilot, who had been captured and suffered imprisonment, smiled and said his thoughts had been exactly the same. "I prayed all the way down."

There is something within the human soul that is naturally inclined to prayer. William James noted this over a hundred years ago. He wondered at all the scientific enlightenment and the discussion about the efficacy of prayer — yet people prayed. "The reason why we do pray is simply that we cannot help praying," he said. Carlyle said something of the same thing: "Prayer is and remains the native and deepest impulse of the soul of man."

It is interesting that Buddhism, a religion without a God, still includes prayer as a dominant force! Confucius, who was agnostic and urged his disciples not to have much to do with the gods, finds a major world religion named after him and millions praying to him.

Abraham Lincoln spoke of this natural impulse when he said, "I have been driven many times to my knees by the overwhelming conviction that I had nowhere else to go; my own wisdom and that of all around me seemed insufficient for the day."

Why this natural impulse? Why pray? Why bother?

Sometimes we pray because there is no other resource available. Like Lincoln, we have come up against the edges of our own resources and come to a dead end. The man in the well who "said the prayin'est prayer ... ever prayed," standing on his head, is another illustration of desperation that drives some people to prayer.

Another, more powerful motivator for prayer is the simple desire to commune with God. Sabatier said, "The history of prayer is the history of religion." Prayer seems bound with the nature of the religious impulse.

So we pray. But what should one expect and exactly how should one pray? When we think of prayer, we think of asking God for something. We think of Supplication. We ask God for a favor. We ask God for a good outcome. Supplication is one form of prayer. There are others. When thinking of prayer, think of the word ACTS.

The "A" stands for Adoration. We praise God. The heart's natural impulse is to praise God for God's greatness and majesty.

The "C" of ACTS stands for Confession — laying our souls before God. Confessing our wrongs and failure to do right. Confession is an important part of prayer.

Then we come to "T" which stands for Thanksgiving. God is the source of every blessing. By giving thanks to God we keep the facts straight. God is the Giver and we are the receivers — all the time. Thanksgiving keeps us from playing God. Thanksgiving keeps us from believing that God owes us anything. There is a by-product of thanksgiving: happiness. The thankful person is a happy person.

Then the final part of ACTS is the "S" of Supplication — asking for something for ourselves or someone else.

Does God answer prayer? Yes. Sometimes not in the way we might expect. Helen Inwood has a little poem titled *Answers* that goes like this:

Answers to prayers
Come in various ways,
Sometimes in minutes,
Sometimes in days.
And some take years
To fully unfold
The harvest of love
And blessings they hold.

Answers to prayers
Come in various forms,
Sometimes in sunlight,
Sometimes through storms.
Some blossom early
And some blossom late
But each one will flower —
Have faith and wait!

God answers all prayer one of three ways: "yes," "no," or "not yet."

In the Bible we see examples of all three answers. The Psalmist writes: "O my God, I cry by day, but you do not answer; and by night, but find no rest." (Psalm 22:2) Moses prayed to enter the Promised Land, but dies on Mount Nebo, his request refused. The patriot lifts his lamentation, ". . . you have wrapped yourself with a cloud so that no prayer can pass through." (Lamentations 3:44) Habakkuk wails, "O Lord, how long shall I cry for help, and you will not listen?" (Habakkuk 1:2) Paul cries out that his "thorn in the flesh" might be removed and it is not. Even our Lord prays in the Garden that the cup might be removed from him but it is not.

God also answers in ways we would not choose. An unknown Confederate soldier wrote:

"I asked God for strength that I might achieve. I was made weak that I might learn humbly to obey.

"I asked for help that I might give greater things. I was given infirmities that I might do better things.

"I asked for riches that I might be happy. I was given poverty that I might be wise.

"I asked for power that I might have the praise of men. I was given weakness that I might feel the need for God.

"I asked for all things that I might enjoy life. I was given life that I might enjoy all things.

"I got nothing that I asked for. Everything I hoped for. Almost despite myself, my unspoken prayers were answered. I, among all men, am most richly blessed."

Our God is wise and can see what is best for us even beyond time. We cannot understand how a loving parent, taken from a young child can be the act of a merciful God. We cannot understand the purpose of prolonged suffering. We cannot comprehend why good, decent people would go without while evil people prosper.

Our God is like a mother whose daughter has asked her to help with her math assignment in school so that she can go to her friend's house for the evening and get a good grade. The wise mother may wish her daughter a good grade and a good time at her friend's house, but will refuse the request because love compels the daughter to do her own math and to learn from the experience. The mother's wisdom and love makes all the difference. The same is true for God.

We pray and receive a wonderful promise. Jesus says: "Ask, and it will be given you; search, and you will find; knock, and the door will be opened for you."

We are bold to pray. We pray in confidence asking for God's will to be done. Let us be a praying people: giving God the Adoration, that sets God apart from us ("Hallowed be your name ..."); Confession, that sets us honestly before God; Thanksgiving, that reminds us of the Source of every blessing; and Supplication for ourselves and others — knowing that God wants us to ask to receive; search to find; knock to open.

Happy praying. This is a wonderful resource from *the* Source.

The Peace

*23. The PEACE is shared at this time or after the Lord's
Prayer, prior to this distribution.*

P. The peace of the Lord be with you always.
C. And also with you.

*The ministers and congregation may greet one another in the
name of the Lord.*

Peace be with you.   Peace be with you.

When I was a kid I hated going to family reunions. I had
an aunt who would grab me and hug me and kiss me! Ugh!
I had learned that as a nice, Germanic boy, one does not kiss
or get kissed. Gestures — sure. Once in awhile a handshake.
But a kiss — no way! This woman was insufferable. She
grabbed me. And deep down inside, so deep I could never have
admitted it as a child, I loved the attention and the gesture.

Four times in the letters of the apostles, Christians are asked
to greet one another with a "holy kiss." The practice was
widespread in the early church. Greeting with a kiss is an
eastern gesture still widely practiced in many parts of the world.
The first Christians were people from the middle-east. They
were accustomed to greeting one another with a kiss. It is not
surprising it should be practiced in the early days of the church
and seen as a "holy" act. As an act of worship, the kiss of
peace went beyond formal greeting — it symbolized the love
that Christians have for one another.

Besides the act of kissing, there's the word "peace." One
Hebrew word most of us know is "Shalom." Jews to this day
greet one another with "Shalom" which, of course, means
"peace." But it means more than that too. The Jews meant
in peace more than mere absence of conflict. "Peace" is a large
word like "snow" for Eskimos. They have many words for
"snow." Most of us know "snow" only as the white stuff that

100

falls from the sky in the winter. The Eskimos define snow with various words that are much more specific than we do in our limited English language. The word "love" in the Bible has more specific meanings than our one word "love." "Peace" is like "snow" to the Eskimos or "love" in the Bible — it is restricted in its English meaning. To the Jewish mind, however, "peace" means absence of conflict, but also abundance of God's grace, material blessings, and harmony within the household. Peace means "wholeness." Peace is "fullness" or "completeness." Peace is a broad word indeed! The richness of that one Hebrew word is the wealth brought to this moment in the Lutheran liturgy and so few know it!

Most of us have at least two strikes against us: We do not understand the biblical-Hebraic concept of the word "peace," and most of us cannot get beyond the normal northern-European hesitancy to show affection — especially physical touching and most especially, kissing! Therefore we have largely done away with the kiss of peace. The kiss has deteriorated into a handshake of peace. Or, in many of our congregations — just an acknowledgment (with no physical touching) of peace.

In some congregations there is a sharing of handshakes. Okay. It's better than nothing. This is not the time for being friendly. This is a sacrificial act. In the handshake of peace, we give up our hostilities and resentment; grudges and anger toward another. We ask God for wholeness for another. We ask God for true "shalom" for our sisters and brothers in the faith. Sometimes the sacrificial offering of a tithe — the sacrificial giving of money — is far easier than giving up our pet resentments and justifications for how right we are and how wrong another is.

In the early church there is evidence that the peace may have been intended as a blessing and a dismissal of those who did not receive the sacrament of Holy Communion. The peace bridged the service of the Word with the service of the Eucharist. Justin Martyr, writing around the year 150 A.D. tells that "We salute one another with a kiss, when we have concluded the prayers" prior to the offering.

Why have the peace end the service for non-communion attenders? Why right before the offering? The significance of having the peace prior to the offering comes from Jesus' admonition in Matthew 5:23-24; "So when you are offering your gift at the altar, if you remember that your brother or sister has something against you, leave your gift there before the altar and go; first be reconciled to your brother or sister, and then come and offer your gift."

Before there can be Holy Communion, there must be reconciliation. Before there can be an honest offering, there must be forgiveness! Peace! Note the importance of the peace. Notice the significance of greeting each other with peace. This is a difficult part of our liturgy.

"What if I cannot forgive?" "What if a brother in the faith has done something so hurtful to me that I cannot dismiss it?" "What if the damaging gossip of a sister has hurt our fellowship so much that there should be no forgiveness?" The simplistic answer would be, keep your money to yourself and do not join in Holy Communion! Keep your money to yourself if you plan to keep your resentments to yourself. Sacrifice. Give up. Forgive. Such is the importance of this moment. Too many pastors simply pass over this moment as a mere formality. Too many lay persons glibly say the words and carry their resentments, anger, and hurt to their graves.

Wonderful reconciliations have taken place in the service as one brother walks across the worship space to an alienated sister and the handshake of peace bridges not only the service, but their lives so that there truly can be a "holy communion" in the fellowship of believers. Forgiveness is supremely important to the Lord Jesus Christ who is present in this moment.

Mark Twain once described forgiveness as "the fragrance the violet sheds on the heel that has crushed it." It truly is divine to forgive. How beautiful true forgiveness is. How wonderful true peace shared in the fellowship can be!

Forgive here — at the peace. Otherwise leave your money in your pocket. Leave the fellowship and forget the communion. Leave now before you betray yourself and actually pray, *Forgive us our sins as we forgive those who sin against us.*

Is forgiving easy? Never! But what peace and joy it brings. Jesus loves you and me enough to do everything in his power to wring that last drop of resentment, bitterness, and anger toward another from our wretched bodies so that we might be free as the beings of light. PEACE.

Chapter
Six

The Offering

What if someone were looking over your shoulder as you gave your offering? What if they took special care to see how much you were giving? Then suppose that the amount you gave and your name were mentioned in public as an example for all people? That happened one day in the temple as Jesus and his disciples observed various people giving money to God. Some people gave large amounts and some gave very small amounts. One particular woman gave a very small sum — two little coins worth less than a penny! And yet this is the person Jesus lifted as an example for all people who identify themselves by his name. We call her gift the "widow's mite."

The woman was a widow. This means her husband, the source of all her well-being in that society, was no longer there to protect and provide for her. Any money she could scratch up was important. And she scratched up everything! Her almost worthless copper coins represented her total income!

We, in our great wisdom, would say, "How foolish!" We would comment, "She needs to look after herself. She needs to take care of herself first. She's got to pay her bills first.'' We would rationalize, ''The religious rulers, those hypocritical priests, scribes and pharisees, probably would not have used her offering well. They would probably squander it.'' We would point to her poverty and say, ''She is not capable of giving. Those two little mites won't make any kind of difference what-so-ever.''

We are so wise in our knowledge of money, aren't we? We all know that you cannot give away everything you have and survive. We all know that you've got to look after yourself and your family first. We all know that if you give, you'll have less; if you keep, you'll have more. We know all about the use of money.

But Jesus, we say, loves us. Jesus is wise. Jesus is son of God. Jesus is part of the Trinity. Jesus wants what is best for us. And Jesus used this widow and her mite as the example of Christian giving.

Jesus does want the best for his followers. Part of having the best is giving. Giving generously is part of what defines us as Christians.

One of the best-selling books on the market today is titled *Wealth 101*. It is not a religious book. And yet the writers say that giving is essential to wealth. They suggest giving the Tithe for purely secular reasons. They wisely describe giving as part of wealth. James Russell Lowell defined wealth back in 1848 when he wrote that it is, ''Not what we give, but what we share, For the gift without the giver is bare.''

It is amusing that secular writers suggest giving and the tithe as an expression of wealth. We in the church had an emphasis on tithing and found enormous resistance to it. ''It's too legalistic!'' pastors said. ''It's too much,'' others replied. ''It's not good Lutheran teaching to talk about the law of tithing rather than God's grace.'' ''I can't give that much.'' Or — ''That's not for me or for my church.'' We resisted talking about the tithe and resisted even more giving the tithe.

And now secular people suggest giving the tithe! Why? Authors John Roger and Peter McWilliams say that giving the tithe is important because it is good business! Giving away 10 percent of what we have gives us a mental and emotional framework of abundance — an attitude that is critical if one is to attract even more wealth into one's life. Futhermore, giving the tithe springs from an attitude of gratitude — one of the essential attitudes for happiness and prosperity.

A Christian mother had taught tithing to her family. Her teen-age son had a paper route earning approximately $10 a week. Each week he thankfully give his tithe of $1. After awhile he got his first regular job, which paid about $100 a week. After two or three weeks, he said to his mother, "It was easy for me to give $1 a week to the Lord; but when I tithe on the $100, I am giving $10 a week. That is hard for me to do. There are a lot of things I could do with that money. I could be saving some of it for college or a car."

His mother replied, "I have a solution. Let's pray and ask God to give you your old job back so you can easily and joyfully give your $1 tithe."

Here was a boy who was learning many lessons from a very wise and caring parent: He was learning how blessed he was to have a good-paying job. He was learning an attitude of gratitude. Futhermore, he was learning to manage his money. Giving a tithe teaches one that money has to be apportioned or else there is never enough. He was learning about abundance and how abundant his life had become. That $10 he put in the collection plate because of his $100-a-week earnings was the best investment he could make for a life of financial security and abundance. Here was a young man who would never have financial problems because he was learning to manage his money wisely.

Finally, and most importantly, he was learning the Source of all blessings and how to give thanks for his abundance by sharing it and returning a portion of it back to God.

Does tithing do all that? Does tithing really make for more abundance and gratitude? Does tithing really teach one how to manage money? Is tithing really an act of faith?

Consider this true story: In the desert area of Nevada, a traveler came across an old, run-down well. He found a rusty tin can tied to the pump; inside was this message written on a piece of faded brown paper:

> *This pump is fixed as of July 1928. I put a new sucker washer in it, but the washer dries out and the pump has got to be primed. Under the white rock I buried a bottle of water. There's enough water in it to prime this pump, but not if you drink some first. Pour in about half and let her soak to wet the leather. Then quick pour in the rest and pump away. You'll git water. When you git watered up, fill the bottle and put it back like you found it for the next feller ... P.S. Don't go drinking the water first! Prime the pump with it, and you'll get all you can hold ... You got to give before you can be give to.*

Probably well over 90 percent of Lutherans don't believe that by giving, we receive the blessings God has promised. How much of God's work has been hindered because we drank from the bottle instead of, by faith, priming the pump? How many people have starved because we have enjoyed our abundance without priming the pump of gracious giving? How many churches have not been built because we just can't believe the note that we have to prime to pump? How many of us have financial troubles because we are limited to the small amount that is in the bottle?

Friends, take the bottle from under the white rock. Pour it on the pump and prime it. And then stand back and let God work the financial blessings that are waiting for you.

So many of us live on a limited attitude of scarcity instead of abundance. This is a world over-flowing with abundance and blessing; wealth beyond measure. But all we see is the little bottle of water and think that's all there is. Giving is the supreme act of faith!

Parents, teach your children to give. Teens — I know you don't have much money, but give your tithe and watch what happens. Those of you raising young families, you are strapped

— give as God has graciously given to you. Some of you are facing major expenses or debt. Prime the pump and let God be God. Seniors, your income is limited — but your blessings are not. Have faith! Prime the pump!

The offering has one more important function: It helps us keep our priorities straight. Life does not consist in the number of things we have. The meaning of life is not in our "net worth." The value of our lives is not tied in a bank roll. Money is a servant. Money is a gift. Money is a blessing. As servant, gift, and blessing, money is wonderful. But when money becomes a god, disaster befalls us.

Jesus tells the story of a man who had plenty. Like us, God had blessed him with enough and more than enough. He said to himself, "What should I do? . . . I will pull down my barns and build larger ones, and there I will store all my grain and my goods. And I will say to my soul, 'Soul, you have ample goods laid up for many years; relax, eat, drink, be merry.' But God said to him, 'You fool! This very night your life is being demanded of you.' " (Luke 12:13-21)

We cannot take any of our things with us when we die. Our material blessings serve us only in this life. I read somewhere once that perhaps the reason we can't take it with us when we die is because it wasn't ours in the first place! I like that. Money and things have their places, but they dare not become our gods. We are lost when they do. The offering helps us put money in its proper perspective — as servant, as gift, and as blessing.

Will you remember this next Sunday? As you receive your pay, set aside from the beginning at least 10 percent. Give it in faith. Give it generously and joyfully. Give it while giving thanks to God for the job you have that pays you. Give it thanking God for your income and numerous other blessings. Give and it shall be given to you.

The Offering is one of the most important parts of the Lutheran service. It is our chance to pray through our actions. It is an opportunity to put our faith to work. It is our chance to truly be God's ambassadors by what we do.

The Great Thanksgiving *(LBW)*
The Common Preface *(LW)*

P: The Lord be with you.
C: And also with you.

Hippolytus was a Roman bishop of the early third century. In his *Apostolic Tradition* we learn a great deal about early Christian worship. He included The Great Thanksgiving in his manual on church order and worship. The dialogue that begins with the salutation is the "preface dialogue" (in *Lutheran Worship* and older liturgies of the Lutheran Church, the Great Thanksgiving is simply called "The Preface.") Here we have one of the oldest and least-changed parts of the liturgy. Dating back nearly 2,000 years, the Great Thanksgiving is a celebration of reverence, adoration, joy and thanksgiving. The Preface, as it is called in *Lutheran Worship*, is exactly that: words introducing the central part of the Eucharist.

P: Lift up your hearts.
C: We lift them to the Lord.

You get the feeling that things are intensifying in this part of the preface — leading to the "Holy, holy, holy ..." Here we lift our hearts. Think about it. How can we "lift" our "hearts?" Obviously this is not a time to take things literally! So what does it mean? Does this mean that we get ourselves into a better mood? Does this mean we become more "light hearted" and jovial? What, exactly, does it mean to lift our hearts?

It means simply that we seek to make room for God. Nothing more; nothing less. This is not the time to elevate our moods. This is the time for setting apart our lives for an encounter with the holy. Even if the sermon has put one to sleep or perhaps roused one's spirit to accomplish gargantuan tasks for the sake of the Gospel, leave that aside for the moment and lift up one's heart to that which is holy: God. The sermon

110

will hopefully have led up to and complemented this moment and the attitude of holiness is already in place.

With this dialogue we accelerate into the special prayer of holiness — the "Preface" itself. Suppose I had a little, 50 cent plastic G.I. Joe figure, an electronic video game, and an expensive sports car. They would all be play things. Would they be of the same value? Of course not. Some would be more special than others. I would think nothing of scratching my little figure. A few scratches on my electronic game would not hinder its performance. But I would be quite particular about my new sports car.

So the dialogue leads us to the special otherness of God. The world "holy" means "set apart." Holy signifies otherness; specialness; God-related and divine things. Here we lift ourselves to that higher plane. Augustine says, "Daily throughout the whole world the human race, with almost one voice, responds that it lifts up its heart unto the Lord." With reverence, adoration, joy and thanksgiving, the church catholic surges in response to the gospel. Hearts are lifted. Here we celebrate the "communion" — the fellowship of the faithful.

Origen, the second century Greek theologian, said that a person must "lift up his soul before lifting up his hands; lift up his mind to God before lifting his eyes, and before standing to pray, lift up his spirit from the things of earth and direct it to the Lord of all." Preparation — the "preface" to the feast to come and preparation to meet the Lord God, heavenly king — that's the action in this dialogue.

P: Let us give thanks to the Lord our God.
C: It is right to give him thanks and praise.

Surely giving thanks is a central element of the Eucharist (which is a Greek word meaning "thanksgiving"). It IS right to give God thanks and praise! God is holy; God is that sacred Other. For the creation to give thanks to the Creator is most "right." Cicero said, "A thankful heart is not only the greatest virtue, but the parent of all other virtues." Talk about approaching holiness and one talks about thanksgiving.

111

Like Christmas, we are tempted to limit our thanksgiving to once a year (if that often). Every year the federal government prints office calendars for the upcoming year. In 1972, someone made a colossal mistake on the calendars for 1973. The mistake had to do with Thanksgiving Day — 1973. The calendar designated November 29th as the holiday, but that was not correct. It should have been when it always is — by presidential proclamation — the fourth Thursday in November. In that year it would have been November 22nd, and not the 29th as the calendar stated.

Being the practical folks they are in the General Services Administration, they chose not to destroy the one million calendars but attach a correction to each. The correction spoke volumes: "Please excuse, but we're giving thanks on the wrong day this year. It's November 22nd."

The Great Thanksgiving invites us to go ahead and give thanks on November 29 and 22 and every other day on the calendar as well! Thanksgiving, like Christmas, is part and parcel of the Christian story. It is essential to the Christian faith!

On a stormy night in 1860 two vessels, one a freighter and the other a passenger ship, collided on Lake Michigan. The *Lady Elgin* carried several hundred passengers. When it began to sink, the people jumped into the water, clinging to whatever floated — even the large bass drum of the ship's orchestra.

As the survivors struggled to shore, people on land waded out into the water to extend a helping hand. One of those participating in the rescue work was a college student named Edward Spencer who was an expert swimmer. He rescued 17 persons. But so great was the strain on his body that he lost his health and spent the rest of his life in a wheelchair.

Many years later this hero was asked what he remembered most about that tragic day. The reply was immediate: "I recall that not one of the 17 persons thanked me for saving his life."

The Christian thanks her or his God for saving her or his life — eternally. It is ingrained. It is a practical necessity. Thanksgiving leads to thanksliving and generosity of spirit.

That generosity is reflected in the liturgy of the Great Thanksgiving.

P: It is indeed right and salutary . . . we praise your name and join their unending hymn:
C: Holy, holy, holy Lord, God of power and might: Heaven and earth are full of your glory. Hosanna in the highest. Blessed is he who comes in the name of the Lord. Hosanna in the highest.

The pastor says "It is indeed right and salutary that we should at all times and in all places offer thanks and praise to you, O Lord . . ." The rest of the prayer fits in with the proper season (*LBW*):

Advent — "You comforted your people with the promise of the Redeemer, through whom you will also make all things new in the day when he comes again to judge the world in righteousness . . ."

Christmas — "In the wonder and mystery of the Word made flesh you have opened the eyes of faith to a new and radiant vision of your glory; that, beholding the God made visible, we may be drawn to love the God whom we cannot see . . ."

Epiphany — "Sharing our life, he lived among us to reveal your glory and love, that our darkness should give way to his own brilliant light . . ."

Lent — "You bid your people cleanse their hearts and prepare with joy for the paschal feast. Renew our zeal in faith and life, and bring us to the fullness of grace that belongs to the children of God . . ."

Passion — We offer thanks and praise to God, "through Christ our Lord; who on the tree of the cross gave salvation to all, that, where death began, there life might be restored, and that he, who by a tree once overcame, might by a tree be overcome . . ."

Easter — ". . . Chiefly we are bound to praise you for the glorious resurrection of our Lord; for he is the true Passover

113

Lamb who gave himself to take away our sin, who by his death has destroyed death, and by his rising has brought us to eternal life ..."

Ascension — We offer thanks and praise to God, "through Christ our Lord; who, after his resurrection, appeared openly to his disciples and, in their sight, was taken up into heaven, that he might make us partakers of his divine nature ..."

Pentecost — We worship the one "who rose beyond the bounds of death and, on this day, as he had promised, poured out your Spirit of life and power upon the chosen disciples ..."

Trinity — "You have revealed your glory as the glory also of your Son and of the Holy Spirit: three persons, equal in majesty, undivided in splendor, yet one Lord, one God, ever to be adored in majesty, undivided in splendor, yet one Lord, one God, ever to be adored in your everlasting glory ..."

Sundays after Pentecost — We adore "Christ our Lord; who on this day overcame death and the grave, and by his glorious resurrection opened to us the way of everlasting life ..."

Weekdays — "It is indeed right and salutary that we should at all times and in all places offer thanks and praise to you, O Lord, holy Father, through Christ our Lord. And so, with the Church on earth and the hosts of heaven, we praise your name and join their unending hymn ..."

Apostles — We offer thanks and praise to the one who "through the great shepherd of your flock, Christ, our Lord; who after his resurrection sent forth his apostles to preach the Gospel and teach all nations, and promise to be with them always, even to the end of the age ..."

All Saints — "In the blessedness of your saints you have given us a glorious pledge of the hope of our calling; that, moved by their witness and supported by their fellowship, we may run with perseverance the race that is set before us and with them receive the unfading crown of glory ..."

In the early church liturgies, the Preface was very lengthy — recounting all the benefits for which we should thank God: the wonders of nature, God's progressive revelation, as well as a commemoration of our Lord's life upon earth, as well as an account of the institution of the Lord's supper. Many of these benefits of knowing God are retained in the Eastern liturgies. Our Lutheran liturgy has dropped the details and retained only the phrase, **"We should at all times and in all places offer thanks and praise ..."**

The seasonally-adjusted part of what the pastor says usually concludes, **"And so, with the Church on earth and the hosts of heaven, we praise your name and join their unending hymn: Holy, holy, holy ..."**

It should be noted that *Lutheran Worship* has retained more detail than the *Lutheran Book Of Worship*. The various Prefaces are, therefore, longer. Also *Lutheran Worship* prints the Prefaces in the worship book whereas they are included only in the *Minister's* edition of the *LBW*.

When I arrived at my first church, fresh out of seminary and with visions of transforming the world with my mighty preaching, compassionate pastoring, efficient ministering, there were fewer than 20 at my first worship service. Over the three years I was at that parish, I had great hopes that the church would grow and flourish in spirit and in numbers. But I had to bump up against reality and face the fact that there were only a few of us on some Sundays — especially in the summer. I found great comfort in the text: "Where two or three are gathered in my name, I am there among them." (Matthew 18:20) The wonderful news is that more than two or three are gathered. The whole "Church on earth and the hosts of heaven," join together in an invisible and inaudible chorus of praise to the living God — even as we lifted our hearts, souls and minds to this same eternal Spirit. The great thread of fellowship ties the whole church catholic together in one, holy communion.

The Great Thanksgiving concludes with the "Holy, holy, holy" (we used to call this the "Sanctus" [Latin for "holy"]). The "Sanctus" is the climax and conclusion of this part of the liturgy. Here the congregation joins the songs of the angels. (See Isaiah 6:3; also Psalm 118:26) The congregation exults as did the crowd when the Lord Jesus entered Jerusalem

115

on Palm Sunday. This "Holy, holy, holy" has been called "the most ancient, the most celebrated, and the most universal of Christian hymns."

The Words Of Institution

In high school physics I remember learning that light is a wave and that light is a particle. "What is it," I wondered. "Is it a wave or is it a particle?" It has been a long time since high school physics, but light remains a mystery — for me at least.

As light is a paradox in the natural world, Martin Luther affirmed some theological paradoxes: a Christian is a saint as well as a sinner. A Christian is totally free to do as she pleases because of the freedom of the Gospel, but totally bound to do acts of love because of the demands of the Gospel. The scripture speaks of similar paradox: The one who would save his life is the one who loses and the one who loses is the one who saves. In living we die; in dying we live. By forgiving the wrongs against us we are forgiven. Being forgiven we can forgive those who have trespassed against us.

We have a similar mystery in Holy Communion. The bread we eat is bread. It does not change substances. It does not become human flesh. Every particle of it is bread. The wine does not change into human blood. It looks, tastes, smells and IS still wine. And yet in the bread we have Christ's body; in the wine we have Christ's blood. Jesus Christ is with us and becomes a part of us in this holy sacrament. Do I understand it? NO! Will I ever comprehend its meaning? Not intellectually. I just know that in the bread and wine, I participate in Christ and he becomes a part of me. I become a "little Christ" as Luther says. I become his presence in the world. I become his loving heart, warm smile, accepting arms, healing hands, good-news-telling-tongue, and message-spreading-feet. This is a mystery that is awe-full. This is overwhelming to a sinner such as myself. How dare I claim to be Christ's presence in this hurting world? And yet I am! Paradox. Mystery.

116

The veil covering the bread and the wine reminds us of the mystery. Hidden, yet revealed. Like so much of Christian thought, the Sacrament of the Altar is a mystery beyond scientific inquiry. I cannot understand it intellectually, but my spirit can comprehend it if only I let it happen.

So, exactly WHAT is happening in this mystery? Luther writes in his *Large Catechism*:

> *It is the true body and blood of the Lord Christ in and under the bread and wine which we Christians are commanded by Christ's word to eat and drink. As we said of Baptism that it is not mere water, so we say here that the sacrament is bread and wine, but not mere bread or wine such as is served at the table. It is bread and wine comprehended in God's Word and connected with it.*[13]

That is a good description of what the sacrament is. Now what does it do? What benefit does it give? Again Luther:

> *We have briefly considered the . . . essence of this sacrament. Now we come to its power and benefit, the purpose for which the sacrament was really instituted, for it is most necessary that we know what we should seek and obtain there. This is plainly evident from the words . . . "This is my body and blood, given and poured out for you for the forgiveness of sins." In other words, we go to the sacrament because we receive there a great treasure . . .*[13]

He goes on to call it "food for the soul" which is given as a "daily food and sustenance so that our faith may refresh and strenghten itself and not weaken in the struggle but grow continually stronger." The new life in Christ, he says, continually suffers opposition and continually develops and progresses.

If the Sacrament is so important, why is it celebrated so rarely in our churches? Most Lutheran churches do not celebrate "daily" (as Luther suggests above). Most don't even celebrate weekly. Why?

I cannot answer that except to say that we limit ourselves by limiting our access to this Sacrament. I would hate to eat just one meal a month. My physical self is important but I consider my spiritual self even more important. Yet I find deep resistance (perhaps it is laziness and a not-too-well-tuned spirituality) within myself.

Who should participate in this Sacrament? Certainly everyone calling him or herself "Christian" (although Luther does note that our freedom under Christ does not make this a new law).

In my first church after graduating from seminary I had a man who was in church nearly every Sunday. But when we celebrated Holy Communion, he was absent (or if he were present, he would not come forward to receive the Sacrament). Why? He told me he did not feel "worthy" of receiving Christ.

It is to such unworthiness that the Sacrament speaks. It was given for sinners like you and me. But I suspect that many of us are hesitant to receive the Sacrament because it forces us to consider our attitudes and behaviors as Christ's representatives on this planet. The only way Christ's ministry of preaching, teaching and healing can be accomplished is through his body — the church (that means you and me). That is a tall order!

In the *Lutheran Book Of Worship* we have three options in the so-called "Words of Institution" of our Lord (*Lutheran Worship* retains only the "Words of Institution"). The first one (rubric 31) is a lengthy prayer which traces the history of God's covenant with his people. The second (rubric 32) contains only the words which Jesus used to bless the bread and wine while celebrating the Passover with his disciples before his crucifixion. The third form (rubric 33) emphasizes the salvation history of God, using words from the third chapter of John's Gospel.

Previous Lutheran worship books (until the Service Book And Hymnal) contained only the words of institution because Luther wanted to get away from the idea that the Sacrament was a sacrifice on our part rather than a sacrament, a giving, on God's part. Earlier Roman Catholic liturgies contained such thought. The prayers associated with the first and third options are entirely appropriate (furthermore, there are additional Words of Institution in the *Minister's Desk Edition* that the presiding minister may choose to use).

Chapter
Seven

The Lord's Prayer

Most people — especially when their backs are against the wall — pray. Why? Fosdick noted that prayer is a natural activity of human life. "Can it be," he asks, that everyone "in all ages and all lands, have been engaged in 'talking forever to a silent world from which no answer comes?' If we can be sure of anything, is it not this — that wherever a human function has persisted, unwearied by time, uncrushed by disappointment, rising to noblest form and finest use in the noblest and finest souls, that function corresponds with some reality?"

Luther approaches prayer from another angle. He says that the second commandment requires us to call upon our God. "It is our duty and obligation to pray if we want to be Christians, just as it is our duty and obligation to obey our fathers and mothers and the civil authorities." In other words we pray because it is commanded.[14] Luther furthermore says we ought to pray because God has promised to hear and answer our prayer.

When his disciples asked Jesus to teach them to pray, he taught them the Lord's Prayer. "Don't be like the hypocrites," he said, "who like to make a show of their piety by their public prayers. Instead, go to your room and shut the door behind you and pray the simple, natural words that come from your mouth." He says, "your Father knows what you need before you ask him." (Matthew 6:8) Then he taught them the prayer most Christians know from heart.

Our Father in heaven. Calling God "Father" can be problematic for some people. Parents can fail so miserably. In a survey of hundreds of children, three phrases emerged as the most popular thing fathers say to their kids. The top response is, "I'm too tired." Next, "We don't have enough money." The third most frequent answer of fathers to their children is, "Keep quiet."

One woman shared her life story with me and I was deeply touched. She had been thrown away as an infant. She told me that her mother had been embarrassed by the child's birth and tried to pretend there was no baby by actually throwing her child in the garbage. "If it hadn't been for the warmth created by the rotting garbage, I would have died before I was found," the woman told me.

She was adopted as an infant and from an early age, her father tormented her with sexual abuse. He seemed to love to create misery for her by taking anything important from her. She had only one pet, a cat she loved deeply, and when her father found out about her attachment to the cat, he shot it in front of her. Such was her relationship with parenthood — especially fathers.

Yet even a person such as this woman, knew something of what Jesus intended when he used the phrase "Our Father ..." The exhaustive poetry she wrote and showed me indicated an almost instinctive knowledge that parents, at least in their ideal, can be loving, protective, caring, nurturing, kind, and everything she did not experience from her father. Jesus tells of our loving, heavenly Father who is everything an ideal dad should be.

A child is not a parent. This prayer begins with a clear distinction of our status. We are not God. That old temptation to be like God is set aside as we pray "Our Father" and not "Our Friend." Our status is childlike — needy and dependent. This is difficult for us self-sufficient creatures to comprehend.

Hallowed be your name. As I write this Halloween is just a few days away. "Halloween" is a contraction for "all hallows even" — the evening before all hallows day (All Saints' Day — November 1). To hallow means to make holy. It is the name that is holy, but we have nothing to do with making it such. The name is holy in and of itself, "but we pray in this petition that it may also be holy with us," Luther says in his *Small Catechism.*

It's that name again. The name that is sacred, other, blessed above all others. The very name we use to curse, swear, and deceive. The very name we ignore when we want what we want. The very name that we forget so frequently.

A pastor wrote in his newsletter:

> *I remember seeing huge letters painted on a rocky cliff beside a highway out west: "Jesus lives" — to which an irreverent hand had added, ". . . in Butte, Montana." I remember seeing these words lettered on a blackened wall beneath a railroad trestle: "Jesus saves" — and again an addition, ". . . at First Federal." And in a washroom at a prominent university these words were penciled large: "Jesus never fails . . . he's got something on the dean."*
>
> *When I see or hear such things, I never know whether to laugh or cry, or shout out in anger. For I do have a queasy feeling about fanatics who paint Jesus' name on rocks. But I am also troubled by the graffiti that tramps with muddy boots on holy ground, making fun of that great name, at which every knee should bow. Somehow, it's sacrilege, and distortion, and mockery.*

Whether it be the name of God our Father or Jesus our brother, we pray in this petition that God's name would be lifted high in a time when neither names nor sacred objects have the meaning they did in biblical times. We pray that God's name become holy to us. As Evelyn Underhill put it: "the Lord's Prayer looks toward a goal in which every action shall be an act of worship; an utterance of the Name."[15]

Your kingdom come. We ask for so much in prayer and so often ask for the wrong thing or things. When we pray for God's kingdom to come, we ask that God would have God's way with us in our living in time and eternity.

There is an old story about a patriarch who died and left three sons to divide what was left of the estate. They had to decide what they wanted after Jenna, the slave took what she wanted. It seems she had served her master well and he left everything to her. Anything left could be divided by the brothers. The eldest got first choice. He chose some land. The next son chose some personal property. But the youngest son chose Jenna.

In asking for God's kingdom, we choose Jenna. We ask for that which really counts. God's kingdom is what really counts.

Your will be done, on earth as in heaven. My father would not let me play on the street when I was young. I'm glad he didn't. Similarly, I submit myself to God's higher purposes and plans knowing and trusting they are best for me, for those near me, and for my world.

Underwood says, "The Name, the Kingdom, and the Will are the things that matter; that their perfection may be manifest on earth as in heaven. Worship is here seen to be in essence a devotedness to God's interests, a movement, an interior disposition of love ..."[16]

The other day I was listening to the theme of a morning news show and singing along: "Oh what a beautiful morning. Oh what a beautiful day. I've got that wonderful feeling, everything's going ..." I hesitated and said, "God's way." I know that's not the way the song goes, but that's the way I felt.

Recently I had tried taking control of my life and was determined to do something that now, in retrospect I see, was utterly stupid! At the time it seemed so right. At that moment it seemed like the thing to do. I had not prayed about it. I had not sought God's will. On a subconscious level I knew God would not approve. So I left God out of the picture and sought my own satisfaction. How foolish of me.

Someone has said that if God really wanted to punish us, God would answer all our prayers in the affirmative. We simply don't have the wisdom, depth, and the maturity of our Creator. Faith means letting go and letting God. Trusting in God's ultimate purposes and goodness means praying for God's will no matter what!

Jesus is the supreme example of this when he prayed in Gethsemane for the cup of suffering to pass from him, never-the-less, "your will be done" he said. How many Gethsemanes does our Lord intend for us? Can you, can I really pray this petition? Can we afford not to pray it? C. S. Lewis said, "The hardness of God is kinder than the softness of men, and His compulsion is our liberation."

The *Gelasian Sacramentary* has this prayer:

> *O Thou who hast taught us that we are most truly free when we lose our wills in Thine, help us to gain that liberty by continual surrender unto Thee, that we may walk in the way which Thou hast prepared for us, and in doing Thy will may find our life, through Jesus Christ our Lord.*

A poem by T. Baird says it well:

> *It is God's will that I should cast*
> *My care on Him each day (1 Peter 5).*
> *He also asks me not to cast*
> *My confidence away (Hebrews 10).*
> *But, oh, how stupidly I act*
> *When taken unaware;*
> *I cast away my confidence*
> *And carry all my care.*

Give us this day our daily bread. This petition speaks of simple food: bread in the present moment: now. I tend to want elaborate gifts from God: a nice car, nice home, secure job, loving family life, healthy bank balance, etc. And I tend to want it for today, tomorrow, and forever.

Living in the moment with the basics seems to be a healthy approach to life. Of the 52 Americans held hostage in Iran, fellow Lutheran Col. Thomas Schaefer, USAF, was the senior military officer. He was accused of being a spy and spent three months in solitary confinement. When asked if his military training helped him survive, he replied that it did. "I know that I had some good survival and anti-terrorist training. That helped — especially the parts regarding surviving on a minimum of food and maintaining your sanity."

"I kept up my exercises four hours a day and came out in better physical shape than I had been in the last 25 years. I read whenever I could, and actually made myself a daily schedule and kept with it. What's more, I applied a basic lesson of survival training — I handled only one day at a time."

Living one day at a time and trusting in God each beautiful day, is the essence of confident faith. Jesus points out that the birds of the air do not worry and neither do the lilies flowering in a radiance brighter than anything Solomon might wear have a care. As God provides for the lowly sparrow and lily, how much more so does this God provide for you and for me one day at a time.

An anonymous poet has written:

> *We cannot change yesterday*
> *That is quite clear*
> *Nor begin on tomorrow*
> *Until it is here*
> *So all that is left for you and for me*
> *Is to make today as great as can be*

Forgive us our sins as we forgive those who sin against us. In 1755, in the midst of an election campaign for seats in the

126

Virginia assembly, 23-year-old Colonel George Washington said something that a hot-tempered little man named Payne considered insulting. Payne promptly knocked Washington down with a hickory stick. Soldiers rushed to Washington's side as he got to his feet to tell them that he would take care of himself. The next day Washington wrote Payne a letter requesting an interview at a tavern. When Payne arrived, he naturally expected a demand for an apology and a challenge to a duel. But Washington was bigger than that. He apologized for the insult and wished Payne well and then offered him the hand of friendship.

The natural human tendency is to take our insults, and our unjustices with vengeance in mind. We wear them like fine costume jewelry. We engrave all injuries done to us in marble as a monument to our pain and justification for whatever actions follow. So the circle of hurt escalates. It grows. Lives are hurt.

The person suffering the greatest hurt from not forgiving is the person not forgiving. It fills the mind with dark imaginings and the body with vile juices. The injury done to us is often far less hurtful than the pain we cause ourselves by holding on to that injury as if it were some dear friend whom we might never see again.

Forgiving comes from two beautiful words: *for* which means, to favor; *giving* which means to give a gift. The person favored most with the gift is the forgiver. The gift is removing the burden of hurt that another has imposed.

There is that beautiful, if questionable, story about Jesus and the woman caught in adultery. "Let anyone among you who is without sin be the first to throw a stone at her." (John 8:7) Then Jesus straightened up, looked around and asked, "Woman, where are they?" (v. 10) Who among us is without sin? Who among us has had to rely on the good will of others for forgiveness?

In this petition we are asking God to do what we do to others. Our actions hurt God and we ask that God might deal

127

with us as we deal with others. In other words if you have a hurt you cannot forgive another, don't say this petition! You want God to forgive you, don't you? Then forgive!

Save us from the time of trial. Trials and temptations come to every one of us. There are times when the problems we face seem overwhelming. It seems that evil has the last word and that we just can't take it any more.

Roland Bainton, in his book *Here I Stand*, tells how Martin Luther, as a father who had known the anguish of losing a dear child, shared his thoughts as he contemplated the scene of Abraham and his son Isaac: "This is what it is to sit in sackcloth and ashes. If he had known that this was only a trial, he would not have been tried. Such is the nature of our trials, that while they last we cannot see to the end ... The father raised the knife; the boy bared his throat. If God had slept an instant the lad would have been dead. I could not have watched. I am not able in my thoughts to follow. Never in history was there such obedience save only in Christ. But God was watching, and all the angels. The father raised the knife, the boy did not wince. The angel cried, 'Abraham, Abraham!' See how divine majesty is at hand in the hour of death. We say, in the midst of life we die. God answers, 'Nay, in the midst of death we live.' " Martin Luther's wife Katie interrupted him once when he was telling this story in family devotions. "I do not believe it. God would not have treated his son like that." "But Katie," said Luther, "He did, He did."[17]

The time of trial strengthens all God's people. In John Steinbeck's classic, *The Grapes of Wrath*, the main characters belong to a family named Joab (Job) who find their true identity when good times are gone. His basic theme is that the more one has the less thankful one tends to be. The itinerant preacher, Jim Casey, puts his finger on it saying, "Maybe the good Lord takes things away from us to get our attention."

Our God will see us through every trial and temptation. God is faithful. We pray that we may also be faithful.

And deliver us from evil. Like it or not, bad things do happen and they happen to every one of us. Evil is real. The Evil

One is real. These are real enemies that each of us has and they are spiritual enemies. They would love to destroy every shred of happiness; every parcel of joy.

The abiding good news of the Gospel is that evil has been defeated. God has the final word! Isn't that wonderful? Of course it is! So, if this is such wonderful news, why is it we don't show it more?

The German philosopher Nietzsche told about the Christians of his acquaintance: "They must look more saved. They must sing better songs, if they want me to believe in their Savior." He had a good point. Christians, if they believed in the triumph of good over evil, would have less fear, fewer worries, diminished anxiety, and better appearances and happier songs with greater enthusiasm!

Martin Luther reflected the victory over evil when he wrote, "When I go to bed, the devil is always waiting for me. When he begins to plague me, I give him this answer: 'Devil, I must sleep. That's God's command. "Work by day, sleep by night." So go away.' If that doesn't work and he brings out a catalog of sins, I say, 'Yes, old fellow, I know all about it. And I know some more you overlooked. Here are a few extra. Put them down.' If he still won't quit and presses me hard and accuses me as a sinner, I scorn him and say, 'St. Satan, pray for me. Of course you have never done anything wrong in your life. You alone are holy. Go to God and get grace for yourself. If you want to get me all straightened out, I say, 'Physician, heal thyself.' ''

God delivers you and me from the evil that comes — every evil. Death and the grave have no power over you and me. Isn't that wonderful?

For the kingdom, the power, and the glory are yours, now and forever. Amen. This conclusion is not in the Lord's prayer but was added much later. It is a doxology to God. The key word here is *Amen.* Amen is found 150 times in the New Testament. Jesus used it uniquely when he wanted to emphasize a point. We see it most often in John's Gospel: "Very truly I tell you ..." *(which in the original language says, "truly, truly ..." ["amen, amen ..."]).* Luther explains it in his *Small Catechism*: " 'Amen, amen' means 'Yes, yes, it shall be so.' " God hears our prayer and promises us an answer.

I had a dramatic, and perhaps coincidental, illustration of this one afternoon in the intensive care unit of the local hospital. Helen had had a severe stroke several days earlier. An electroencephalogram reading indicated that the stroke had virtually killed her brain. But her heart kept beating and an artificial respirator kept her lungs functioning. The family had to make a decision of whether or not they should "pull the plug." They decided unanimously to do so but they wanted to gather one more time around Helen's bed and say their final farewells and prayers. I was asked to be present. When it seemed that everyone was finished, I invited the family to join hands around Helen. I took her left hand and her husband was on her right as we formed a caring circle around her that afternoon. The family prayed various petitions. When all had finished, I said a few words and led the family in praying the Lord's Prayer. When we got to "Amen" there was a buzz from one of the machines. It took me a moment to realize that the buzz was the electrocardiogram giving a flat reading. Helen's heart had stopped precisely when we said "Amen." It was as if she heard us and the Lord had heard the family's prayers. The plug never had to be pulled. Helen was asleep peacefully in the Lord. Her strong-beating heart finished when we concluded the prayer. "Amen, amen — yes, yes, it shall be so." I was moved to tears.

Our Lord has taught us a beautiful and meaningful prayer. It is no wonder that this prayer has been in use in the Christian church from the very beginning. It says so much and is so meaningful, especially when we turn off the mental tape that is on automatic rewind and take a moment to look at the meaning of the thought and words.

This, by the way, is one reason why the prayer should be read and not merely said from memory. It helps us focus on the meaning rather than the words. This is also why I like to use different versions of the Lord's Prayer even though most lay people resist this with a vengeance. In my opinion it should be substance over form. There is no value in even the most pious and beautiful of "empty phrases."

Amen!

Chapter
Eight

The Communion

We approach the Lord's Table with love and respect. Each communicant should examine herself or himself to see what the Sacrament is leading one to be or to do. Paul writes in 1 Corinthians 11:28-29: "Examine yourselves, and only then eat of the bread and drink of the cup. For all who eat and drink without discerning the body, eat and drink judgment against themselves." One might ask, "Am I harboring a grudge against anyone?" "Am I working hard to forgive those who have sinned against me?" "Do I believe this is Christ's body and blood?" "Am I intent on being Christ's presence in this world?"

In earlier times communicants fasted before participating in the body and blood of Christ. Probably not many actually prepare this way today, but those who do find deep meaning and spiritual value in such preparation. Quiet prayer before worship is very useful. The prayers at the front of the *Lutheran Book Of Worship* and *Lutheran Worship* are useful for preparation. Focusing on the meaning of the hymns sung prior to

Holy Communion can be helpful. Likewise, quiet time in prayer before and perhaps after receiving the Sacrament is excellent preparation for the Lord.

Our preparation dare not be such a fearsome thing that it might keep one from the Communion; and neither ought it be such a casual thing that it is completely overlooked. There is great value in preparation and examination of oneself. As Luther said in the *Small Catechism*: "Fasting and bodily preparation are a good external discipline, but he is truly worthy and well prepared who believes these words: 'for you' and 'for the forgiveness of sins.' On the other hand, he who does not believe these words, or doubts them, is unworthy and unprepared, for the words 'for you' require truly believing hearts."

In the Roman Catholic church the laity receive the Communion at the rail outside the chancel. Many protestant churches receive the Sacrament individually, at their pews. But Lutherans direct people to come forward, enter the chancel and come to the altar — the symbol of the presence of God. We even call this "The Sacrament of the Altar." There is significance to what we do. The Communion is exactly that — a "communion" shared with others. That is why we go beyond seeing the Sacrament as a private act for the individual in the pew. Holy Communion is also a means our Lord uses to speak of God's grace. The nearness of God is our reason for coming to the altar. We call Holy Communion and Holy Baptism "means of grace."

In the early church, the communicants stood to receive the Sacrament. Many Lutheran churches retain this practice. After the 12th century kneeling became the generally accepted way of receiving throughout the western church. We receive in a state of humility and reverence. That is why sitting is not acceptable (except, of course, for those unable to stand or kneel). Kneeling is most appropriate during the penitential seasons of Advent and Lent; standing is most proper during Easter. The ancient church even forbade kneeling during the 50 days of Easter joy.

134

For years theologians argued for the common cup as a symbol of Christian fellowship and unity. But laity in most of our churches have demanded the individual cups. Our American obsession with hygiene is the primary drive for the cups even though various chemical and bacteriological studies have shown the individual cup to be quite safe. If the common cup is not used, individual cups can be filled from a chalice with a pouring lip to preserve the significance of the "one cup."

Many congregations use a common loaf of bread to symbolize the unity Paul spoke of when he said, "Because there is one bread, we who are many are one body, for we all partake of the one bread." (1 Corinthians 10:17) The word Paul uses for bread denotes common bread used at that time. Using leavened bread gives the Sacrament more of an association with what we commonly identify as bread. The bread used by our Lord at the Passover meal was unleavened bread. That is why many congregations use wafers made of unleavened bread. Wafers are also easy to handle and store. A further advantage of wafers is that there are no crumbs. But many people have an unfavorable bias against the commercial wafers used in the majority of our churches. Ideally home-made unleavened bread baked in a loaf like pita bread would best symbolize the unity of the Sacrament.

The celebrant distributes the bread and says, "The body of Christ, given for you." The assisting minister may be a lay person. He or she may distribute the wine saying, "The blood of Christ, shed for you." The recipient would find the Sacrament most meaningful by listening to the phrases, ". . . given for you . . . shed for you" and knowing for sure that Christ was given for him or her. To reinforce that, the communicant should say "Amen" upon receiving each element.

I attended a service recently where I was not leading. It was a wonderful service and the Gospel came through very clearly. I felt God's love. When the benediction was pronounced, I heard the word "you" and realized, for the first time in a long time, that meant me! So here, the body and blood of Christ is for you! You are most precious to God. This Sacrament affirms your value.

135

The bread is usually placed in the communicant's hand. Tertullian, in the second century, and Cyril of Jerusalem, in the fourth affirm this practice. Cyril describes the method: "making the left hand a throne for the right, and hollowing the palm of the right to receive the Body of Christ." During medieval times the priest placed the wafer directly on the communicant's tongue. Until fairly recent times, the common practice in the Lutheran church was to place the bread directly in the mouth. Again, modern hygienic knowledge has probably been the force to place the bread in the communicant's hand.

Some churches practice intinction by dipping the bread in the common chalice. Thus both bread and wine are received simultaneously.

Lamb Of God

The "Lamb of God" is listed in the *Lutheran Book Of Worship* and *Lutheran Worship* liturgy as an option along with other hymns. In earlier liturgies, this hymn was considered standard. The beautiful, meditative communion hymn was introduced into the liturgy by Pope Sergius I, about 700 A.D. It is based on John 1:29, when John the Baptist says, " 'Here is the Lamb of God who takes away the sin of the world.' "

It reminds us of the Kyrie with its emphasis on Mercy and Peace. It was, after all, God's mercy and peace that prevailed when God's people were in Egypt. The Angel of Death came upon the land, but wherever the blood of the sacrificial, pure lamb was smeared over the doorposts of the house, the first born was spared — the angel *passed over*. We get the word *Passover* from this dramatic example of God's tremendous mercy and the peace it brings.

Jesus is the Lamb of God who was sacrificed for our benefit so that death might pass over us. It is the blood of Jesus we drink. It is his body we eat.

Singing hymns during the distribution is the prevailing practice in our Lutheran churches. Luther's German Mass calls for such action. But some congregations — especially those gifted with a spiritually discerning organist — find soft church melodies played on the organ an aid during distribution of the sacrament. Various choral and instrumental music may be skillfully used here as well. Silence also can be a beautiful and meditative aid in distributing the elements. On days of penitential occasions such as Ash Wednesday and Holy Week, silence may best communicate the solemnity of the calendar. When the congregation is not involved in singing hymns, there is a temptation for people in the pews to stare at communicants. This bothers self-conscious people and may be a hindrance to their receiving the Sacrament. Certainly such boorish behavior epitomizes what Paul spoke of when he reminded the Corinthians that their gatherings may actually cause more harm than good. If silence is used, the congregation must use it for something other than the scrutiny of communicants.

Dismissal

38. *After all have returned to their places, the minister may say these or similar words.*

P: The body and blood of our Lord Jesus Christ strengthen you and keep you in his grace.
C: **Amen**

Sometimes each table is dismissed with these words, but to convey the unity or the "communion" of the Sacrament, it would be best if the whole congregation is dismissed simultaneously and respond together, "Amen." Continuous distribution of the Lord's Supper in a smooth and orderly fashion enhances the sense of community our Lord desires.

The Dismissal is listed as a "may" rubric because it stems from pre-Reformation days when it was a formula for dismissing each communicant. The Holy Communion itself is a blessing and no further blessing is needed. Furthermore, the benediction at the end of the service is coming.

137

Whether or not the Dismissal is used, each communicant will want to return to her or his seat in an attitude of prayer and devotion after having received the body and blood of the Lord. Some excellent pre- and post-communion prayers are found at the front of *Lutheran Worship* and the *Lutheran Book Of Worship*. Psalms, hymns and other prayers may be used to further aid in personal reflection upon receiving the blessed Sacrament.

Post-Communion Canticle

When the disciples and the Lord Jesus had finished their last supper together, they sang a hymn and proceeded to the Mount of Olives (Matthew 26:30). We, too, sing a hymn. Two are listed in the Lutheran worship liturgies but others may be sung in their place.

"Thank the Lord and sing his praise . . ." is a beautiful and fitting canticle to be sung on festive occasions. How else does one respond to the grace received in the Eucharist? Thanks, praise, peace come from a heart refreshed with the Bread of Life, Jesus Christ. It is inappropriate during Lent because of the Alleluias.

Someone has noted that the greatest saint in the world is not the one who prays most or fasts with greater discipline; it is not the one who gives the most generously, or has the greatest temperment. The greatest saint is not the one who is most chaste or just. The greatest saint is the one who is always thankful to God and receives everything as an instance of God's goodness and has a heart always ready to praise God for all the blessings great and small. Oliver Wendell Holmes said it like this: "If one should give me a dish of sand, and tell me there were particles of iron in it, I might look with my eyes for them, and search for them with my clumsy fingers, and be unable to find them; but let me take a magnet and sweep it, and now it would draw to itself the most invisible particles by the power of attraction! The unthankful heart, like my

138

finger in the sand, discovers no mercies; but let the thankful heart sweep through the day, and, as the magnet finds the iron, so it will find in every hour some heavenly blessing: only the iron in God's sand is gold.''

The song of ancient Simeon is the second and more traditional Lutheran option. *Lutheran Worship* lists it exclusively in Divine Service I. Mary and Joseph were pious Jews. For seven days, after giving birth, a woman was considered "unclean" and needed to remain in ceremonial isolation for another 33 days. The parents also had to bring their child to the Temple for the rite of presentation. An animal was presented for sacrifice of the first-born male child as a substitute for sacrifice of the child himself. Mary and Joseph were in the temple for ritual purposes. When Simeon saw the infant Jesus in the Temple with his parents, he took the child in his arms and sang, "Lord, now you let your servant go in peace . . .'' (Luke 2:29-32) We, too, can depart in peace because we have seen the Lord. "Taste and see that the LORD is good," the Psalmist exults. (Psalm 34:8)

Sometimes it is a sobering experience to complete this sentence, "Before I die . . .?" Thinking about the finality of life puts things into a perspective that sometimes is quite uncomfortable and is always serious business. Simeon had thought about it and his one wish was to see "the salvation which you have prepared in the sight of ev'ry people: a light to reveal you to the nations and the glory of your people Israel." Now he could die in peace.

We also can depart in peace because we have not only seen the Light Simeon wished to see, but have also tasted the goodness of the Lord. We are reminded of how much more blessed we are than even the great Simeon.

Prayer

There are three post-communion prayers in the *Lutheran Book Of Worship*. The first one, which begins, "We give you thanks, almighty God . . . ,'' is from Luther's German Mass of 1526.

The second prayer, "Pour out upon us the spirit of your love . . . ," is a post-communion prayer for Easter from the Roman Missal.

The third prayer, "Almighty God, you gave your son . . . ," is a new translation from the second Sunday after Easter in the 1549 *Book Of Common Prayer*, of the Church of England.

Lutheran Worship lists two post-communion collects:

> *We give thanks to you, almighty God, that you have refreshed us through this salutary gift, and we implore you that of your mercy you would strengthen us through the same in faith toward you and in fervent love toward one another . . .*

Or:

> *O God the Father, the fountain and source of all goodness, who in loving-kindness sent your only-begotten Son into the flesh, we thank you that for his sake you have given us pardon and peace in this sacrament, and we ask you not to forsake your children but always to rule our hearts and minds by your Holy Spirit that we may be enabled to serve you constantly . . .*

The Blessing

41. Silence for reflection
42. The minister blesses the congregation

P: Almighty God, Father, + Son, and Holy Spirit, bless you now . . . and forever.

OR

P: The Lord bless you and keep you.
The Lord make his face shine on you and be gracious to you.
The Lord look upon you with favor and give you peace.
C: Amen

A physician of Philadelphia left his house early one morning, hurrying down the street. He noticed along the way a very peculiar-looking man whose gaze seemed to penetrate the doctor's being.

Being a kind and polite man, the physician smiled gently, raised his hat, and passed by the man. Then he heard a loud shot from behind him. Turning around to the source of the noise, he found the stranger had just shot the person behind him. The police investigation later revealed that the killer had just left his home with the insane purpose of shooting the first man he met. The physician was the first man, but his kind face and benign smile had thrown the killer off his guard, and the next passerby got the bullet intended for him. That smile saved his life!

Who has not been lifted by a smile? A smile — even a feigned and insincere one — has a tendency to melt the human heart. The Lutheran service ends with a smile. A wonderful smile. A blessed smile. A gracious smile. **"The Lord make his face shine on you,"** it says. Then the benediction repeats, **"The Lord look upon you with favor."** Both of these are ways of saying, God smiles at us! The shining face and wonderful favor of the Lord goes with us at the end.

Again we hearken to the Tinity. The minister asks that God the **"Father . . . Son . . . Holy Spirit"** would **"bless you."** the **"you"** here is plural — all the people who are before the minister.

The other benediction, which is the second one listed in the *Lutheran Book Of Worship* is the so-called Aaronic benediction (Numbers 6:24-26) which is fairly unique to Lutherans. It is from the Old Testament. It is the only benediction commanded by God. The Lord commanded, by way of Moses, that Aaron and his sons bless the Israelites with these words. Then verse 27 says, "So they shall put my name on the Israelites, and I will bless them."

The word "benediction" comes from two Latin words: "*bene*" meaning "good" and "*diction*" meaning "word." So a benediction is a good word. The good word is the way we end a Lutheran service. The good word from the minister is that God would be with you. Remember, we get the English "good-bye" as a contraction of the same.

More than words are implied. The very smile of God is ours. That is more than mere words could express. The benediction may be a "good word" for us, but the action of God's face shining upon us is a blessed thought. To think that we end with a smile. That is grace, isn't it?

A: Go in peace. Serve the Lord.
C: Thanks be to God.

The service doesn't end — it goes on in another form: service. We depart to serve. Some churches have a sign above the main entrance of the church, on the inside, which says, "Servant's Entrance." What looks like an exit is really an entrance. What looks like the end of the service is really the beginning. We end with thanks to God.

Many congregations have a hymn following the benediction or they prolong the service with quiet music while the candles are extinguished. This "wraps it up," we might say, and gives closure to the service. But perhaps such post-conclusion exercises hinders us from seeing the service as not concluding but continuing in our service to God and each other? St. Augustine said, "When that great Sacrament has been partaken a thanksgiving concludes all." Earlier services show a quick end to the service as our service in life continues.

Conclusion

The people of God have encountered the holy in an effective worship service. God was present. The sacred; the Other has spoken and the people of God have heard. They now return to the world they are called to serve. The pastor, the liturgist, and the musicians have asked to be instruments of God and God has used them effectively. The building, the bells, the stained glass windows, the scents, sounds, and sights of the Holy have moved the people of God into a world of grace and service.

The service was not necessarily entertaining or enjoyable (although it may have been). The worship the people have experienced was not thrilling and fun (although it may have been). It was not comfortable and predictable (although it may have been). It did not provide for peoples' fellowship needs (although it may have). The service lifted the participant from the ordinary to the sacred. God and God's presence seemed somehow more real.

An old miner explained to a visitor, "I let my mules spend one day a week outside the mines to keep them from going blind." The worship service does that to us. In worship we have seen the Light of the world. That reality keeps us from going blind to the deeper realities of life and existence. The service has opened our eyes again.

Sources

The sources for the liturgies quoted are from *Lutheran Worship*, copyright © 1982 Concordia Publishing House. Used by permission from CPH.

The other liturgy is reprinted from *Lutheran Book Of Worship*, copyright © 1978, by permission of Augsburg Fortress.

1. From *Ceremony And Celebration* by Paul H. D. Lang. Copyright © 1965 Concordia Publishing House. Used by permission from CPH. (St. Louis: Concordia, 1965).

2. All scripture quotations are from the *New Revised Standard Version Of The Bible*, copyright 1989 by the Division of Christian Education of the National Council of the Churches of Christ in the USA.

3. Reprinted from *A Manual On Worship* by Paul Zeller Strodach, copyright © 1946 Muhlenberg Press. Used by permission of Augsburg Fortress. (Philadelphia: Muhlenberg, 1946, p. x).

4. Saffen, Wayne, *The Second Season*. (Reprinted by permission of the author).

5. Reprinted from *The Lutheran Liturgy* by Luther Reed, copyright © 1947 Muhlenberg Press. Used by permission of Augsburg Fortress. (Philadelphia: Fortress Press, 1947, p. 279).

6. Reprinted from *Manual On The Liturgy: Lutheran Book Of Worship*, copyright © 1979, by permission of Augsburg Fortress. (Pfatteicher, Philip H. and Messeril, Carlos R., *Manual On The Liturgy: Lutheran Book Of Worship*, Minneapolis: Augsburg Publishing House, 1979, pp. 214-215).

7. As quoted by Pfatteicher, Philip H., & Messerli, Carlos R., *Manual On The Liturgy Lutheran Book Of Worship*, Augsburg: Minneapolis, 1979, p. 20.

8. Reed, Luther, *The Lutheran Liturgy*, Philadelphia: Fortress Press, 1947, p. 298.

9. Buechner, Frederick, *Wishful Thinking: A Theological ABC*, New York: Harper & Row, 1973, p. 79.

10. Reed, p. 306.

11. *Church Music Memo*, Spring 1977.

12. Barclay, William, *The Apostles' Creed For Everyman*, New York: Harper & Row, 1967.

13. Reprinted from *The Book Of Concord*, edited by T. G. Tappert, copyright © 1959 Fortress Press. Used by permission of Augsburg Fortress. (Luther, Martin, *The Large Catechism* (The Book Of Concord, Theodore G. Tappert, ed. [Philadelphia: Fortress Press]), 1959, p. 447 & 449).

14. Ibid. p. 421.

15. Underhill, Evelyn, *Worship*, New York: Harper & Row, 1936 (1957 edition), p. 226.

16. Ibid. p. 227.

17. From *Here I Stand: A Life Of Martin Luther*. Copyright renewal © 1978 by Roland Bainton. Excerpted by permission of the publisher, Abingdon Press. (New York, Nashville: Abingdon-Cokesbury Press: New York, p. 369-370).